D0732987

THE FRAGILE FACE OF GOD

THE FRAGILE FACE OF GOD

*A true story about light, darkness, and
the Hope beyond the veil*

LEEANN TAYLOR

The Fragile Face of God
Copyright © 2013 LeeAnn Taylor

All rights reserved. No part of this book may be reproduced in any form or by any means, electronic, mechanical, photocopying, scanning, or otherwise, without permission in writing from the publisher, except by a reviewer who may quote brief passages in a review. For information on licensing or special sales, please contact:

Dunham Books
63 Music Square East
Nashville, Tennessee 37203

Trade Paperback ISBN: 978-1-939447-15-9
Ebook ISBN: 978-1-939447-16-6

Printed in the United States of America

TABLE OF CONTENTS

For my mother, Carol.
Our hearts are one.

"What is to give light must endure burning."
~Victor Frankl

PREFACE

Through the ages, man has sought the Light.

For millennia, we have pursued it tirelessly, searching the mystical realms and unseen arenas of mankind's deepest longings. In our quest, we have built shrines, temples, sanctuaries, monasteries, and even climbed the highest mountains to commune with deity. In the flame of a burning bush, in the belly of a whale, on a dusty road to an ancient city—through impassible paths have we travailed. But in all our searchings, we have failed to see the holy ground before our very eyes; we walk it now. In our elaborate imaginings of divinity and its power, we have neglected to see that very power within ourselves. We have been looking for evidence of the Light in all the wrong places. It is here, within us.

Through our very lives, in our very homes, and upon this very moment, we are uncovering evidence of the Light. It may not read like an ancient scroll or have the panache of an eloquent discourse, but like a sheath of ageless hope, it surrounds us, compelling us to wonder and question and believe. We are all on this journey, and whether we encounter hope, or despair, will be determined by how we engage this Light. It rests patiently aside, awaiting our trust to bring it forward.

We will now step into the darkness where the everlasting flame burns in the heart of the human spirit. It is here, against a black backdrop, where it shines brightest. And it is here where the indomitable soul of humankind rises triumphant.

PART ONE

Little Girl with Stars in Her Eyes

CHAPTER ONE
A Prayer for Death

My prayer pierced the silent darkness of my bedroom, barely a whisper.

"Please, help me die."

I shut my eyes and tried to feel something, but I felt nothing. *What would my children think if they knew? What would my husband, who lay sleeping just inches away, think?* Friends and family told me I was amazing, even heroic. But I knew differently. I was no hero.

I wanted to feel my mother's arms holding me tight like I was eight years old again—reaching out to me one last time with the power of her love.

"Help me die before it's too late. Before I do something terrible . . ."

CHAPTER TWO
Alive in Hope

I had stars in my eyes from day one. Inspired by the throb of Tinseltown pulsating just north of our home in Southern California, I imagined myself in movies and on the stage, a bright starlet with a handsome husband. A vivid daydreamer of all things glamorous, I even roped in my little sister to perform elaborate plays with me for the neighborhood kids each week, selling tickets paid for with candy bars. At school, I played a dramatic game of cowboys and Indians, with the covered wagon and stagecoach on our playground serving as the scenery. My best friend and I cried for help from the evil villain; we were exotic Indian maidens tied to the covered wagon as our brave cowboys came to rescue us.

Life was my movie, and I was its star.

Beautiful things and beautiful people fascinated me. Dressed in my mother's white velvet nightgown, I pranced around the house primping like a golden-age film icon. When alone, I posed in front of my mirror—clad in garage sale stilettos and neon orange lipstick—the very portrait of sophistication. As my bedroom curtains parted, there I was—poised on the stage of my windowsill, hairbrush-microphone in hand—shining for my imaginary audience. I was starry-eyed and giddy, and my world was full of wonder.

Music and encouragement filled our home like tandem mentors igniting the flame of my creative spirit. My dad, Lemoyne, was a jazz musician playing gigs on the weekends while teaching junior high school band during the week. I grew up captivated by his stories of playing with musical greats like The Carpenters and Frankie Valli. He had even been in a beatnik rock band in the sixties, complete with mock turtlenecks, satin suits, and a Beatles haircut. I pictured throngs of fans cheering at the stage during those concerts. That's where *I* wanted to be.

My mother, Carol, was also a musician. She played jazz concert band music and loved the clarinet. She had played since high school and was also proficient on the saxophone, oboe, and flute. She even composed original songs.

The music in our home served as a colorful backdrop for my vivid daydreams, and the encouragement was a powerful impulse. Being the daughter of two musicians, I often found myself in the embrace of dramatic compositions such as *Peter and the Wolf* or *Moonlight Sonata*, my mother's personal favorite, which she often played on her clarinet. This haunting melody frightened me in the most longing and beautiful way. It was made more vivid by the foreboding statuette of Beethoven which commanded our living room. The song swept me away to a world of my own, wrought with dashing heroes and brave heroines.

I was loved and nurtured in my mother's arms, a safe place for a little girl. But the place I felt most special was lying beside her in the warm baths she often took after a long day's work. These baths were lingering respites of repose, little private escapes allowing me to experience a rare and intimate side of my mother. Silent and weightless in the water, we floated for hours like angels quietly adrift. I felt treasured in those moments as she peered into my eyes with that glimmer that was her love—that spark of infinite but unspoken truth. I felt as if we truly became one.

My mother was young and petite with short brown hair and soft blue eyes. Her spirited influence was a source of strength to me and to everyone who knew her. She was just eighteen when she married my dad. They met in college where she studied to become a music teacher. My dad was a student-teacher at the time, and was eight years her senior. He was much more pragmatic and serious, a contrast which often clashed with her playful, romantic side, infusing their relationship with drama. She went into their marriage with big career plans and a strong maternal instinct—two potentially opposing forces indicative of her visionary nature. He went into their marriage with a perfectly practical outlook, in no hurry whatsoever to start a family. But five years into their marriage, my mother's secret decision to stop taking the pill changed all that.

Perhaps it was my mother's inner fire subconsciously influencing me, but I was aflame with all the ambitious energy a little girl could muster. Under my mother's free-spirited, sometimes stubborn, yet always creative hand, my dreams flourished. Our home was filled to the brim with her handmade treasures such as colorful wooden trains, hand-painted ceramic birds, and ornately decorated picture collages, fostering my love for beauty from a young age. The smell of her gardenia perfume—her favorite flower—permeated her bedroom and everything she wore. Pale pinks and greens and purples colored the walls of our small 1970s suburban home. The cheerful environment of my bright yellow bedroom was also a reflection of her artistic expression and was her gift to me. It created the perfect setting for my illustrious dramatics and enlivened me with optimism.

I was an idealist in an ideal world, and I was infectiously happy. We had found a little slice of heaven in our corner of the universe.

Then, when I was six years old, my mother discovered a lump in her breast. Her doctor assured her that she had as much chance of winning the Irish Sweepstakes as she did of having cancer; she was only twenty-nine and otherwise healthy at the time. However, a biopsy soon revealed that my mother indeed had breast cancer—*progressive*. Our lives were suddenly swept into a whirlwind. She immediately underwent a mastectomy and began witnessing the harsh effects of chemotherapy, a cruel intruder to our perfect little home. The smell of antiseptic needles and medicines filled the air, replacing the scent of my mother's sweet perfumes and lotions. Bottles of prescription drugs with strange names I couldn't pronounce lined our medicine cabinet and counters. One morning I entered her bedroom and heard retching in her bathroom. I walked over to her bed where large clumps of light brown hair covered her pillow. I was afraid. I turned to the bathroom and saw her leaning over the sink. Blood ran down the drain.

My mother was an elementary grade school teacher, her life's passion and the fulfillment of a lifelong dream. Greatly loved by her students and highly esteemed by her peers, she had made great contributions to the inner-city school where she taught, including composing the school's first song and designing its mascot. She worked hard to acquire her teaching credentials while raising two daughters, and she didn't let the cancer slow her down. After her mastectomy and a brief convalescence, she went right back to work.

It had always been my privilege to join her in the mornings while my little sister slept. My mother's bedroom was the epitome of feminine fascination. She selected fancy little outfits for me, often with colorful details she had lovingly sewn onto them. She dolled me up, fussing over my hair until it was just right and even putting a little makeup on me. Then I helped her dress for work, including fastening her bra in the back, clasping her necklace, and zipping up her mini-dress. Short skirts, long necklaces, and high-heeled shoes were her standard favorites, often in pale pinks, dark purples, or pea greens. Once dressed, I watched her apply her makeup and style her hair.

After the cancer, however, there were new duties and details which became part of our routine. I now helped position her artificial breast form in her bra. It was a squishy ball of gel, flesh-toned and soft, like the fake skin on my baby doll. Because my mother was now bald from the chemotherapy, I also helped her put on her new wig, fastening it securely with my small fingers to make it look as natural as possible.

As we zipped and fastened and curled, my mother instilled in me the importance of independence, of following my dreams, and believing in myself.

"LeeAnn, make sure you never have to rely on anyone," she often told me. "You need to take care of yourself and be independent. Do all the things you love in your life." And then she would add, "It's important, my little porcelain doll."

She listened patiently as I shared grand ideas for my starlit future. Her attention and care during those early mornings made me feel supremely important and greatly loved.

Our cherished morning ritual always concluded with a steaming cup of tea, infusing our small house with the sweet aroma of cloves and orange spice. I felt so grown-up sipping from my mother's favorite china tea cup and sitting like a real lady at the breakfast table. She held my confidence in the hollow of her hand and with gentle wisdom nudged me forward.

One day shortly following her mastectomy, I sat with my mother on her bed and asked if I could see her scar. It represented this strange thing called cancer which had changed our lives so abruptly, and I was curious to see what it looked like. My mother carefully removed her blouse and slipped off her bra. A diagonal line stretched across her chest where her breast had been and made little indents where the stitches were. I reached out my hand to touch it. I sensed it might have been a little scary for her to let me do this, but she let me anyway. I slowly ran my small fingers delicately over the prickly bumps. Bendy black threads jutted out from her flesh in symmetrical shapes and poked my skin. I looked at her other breast, whole and full and perfect, then back at the bumpy pink line under my fingertips. I didn't say a word. Neither did she.

I watched my mother grow dramatically sicker through the next two years. She held up her hand one time, and I could see it trembling. All the color was gone from her face, and she didn't laugh much anymore. She became occasionally distant from us, and the warm baths she and I had once shared were discontinued. She developed another cancerous lump, in her throat, which had to be removed. My dad was now required to administer her medication at home, a task that made him cringe. The process required him to inject chemotherapy chemicals into a bottle of grape juice. My sister and I watched every morning as my mother drank down the entire bottle. Other times my dad injected the needle directly into her arm. She was ultimately unable to work and spent months on the couch wrapped up in a blanket.

December came, and our family took a long-planned skiing vacation up to the mountains of Utah. My mother felt confident she could make the trip. We arrived at the designated location after dark, but were unable to find my uncle who had reserved a cabin for both of our families. We searched for hours in the snow and were finally forced to spend the night in our Volkswagen camper. Temperatures plummeted that night, and my mother's condition deteriorated rapidly. Her breathing became labored, and she grew significantly weaker. By morning, my uncle found us, but my mother was unable to walk and had to be carried into the cabin.

A towering Christmas tree, complete with ornaments and sparkling lights, stood tall in one corner of the cabin, and colorfully wrapped gifts were stacked around it. An over-sized fireplace warmed the room with the fragrant smell of pine. My relatives all came together to greet us for the holiday gathering we had come to spend with them.

A few days later, however, as we sat around the tree, my dad announced that our family would be leaving early. My mother's condition had not improved. I was so disappointed and, like any selfish child, I made a small scene, pouting and complaining that Christmas would be ruined. I even dropped my head in fake tears to show my dismay. After a moment, the room fell silent, and only the sound of weeping could be heard. But it was coming from my mother.

"I'm sorry," she wept, "I didn't mean to ruin Christmas for anyone. I don't want to ruin Christmas. I'm so sorry."

I felt the searing shame of my selfish actions. We returned home the next day.

* * * * * * *

One evening just before Christmas, my dad called me over to the couch and asked me to hold up my arm next to my mother's arm. His fears were confirmed: her skin had turned yellow, which was a sign that the cancer had reached her liver. At the time, I didn't understand the implications of this.

Christmas morning arrived, but my mother was too weak to get out of bed. My dad brought my little sister and me out to our front room. Our Christmas tree sparkled in the twilight, dazzling us with its red and green glass ornaments and thick, gold tinsel. Four homemade stockings with our names embroidered on the front hung from the brick mantle, stuffed with several small gifts for each of us. With all the color and goodies that filled the room, I should have been excited. But a strange stillness was in the air.

Quietly, the three of us began opening presents. A few minutes later, my mother came walking out of the bedroom. She was pale and wrapped up in her usual blanket, but she put on a smile and sat down on the couch. My sister and I jumped up and threw our arms around her in a giggling series of hugs. Somehow she had the strength to join us in those joyful moments that day. We shared gifts, welcomed relatives, laughed like we hadn't laughed in a long time, and celebrated Christmas together—as if we were all going to live forever.

Sometime during the night, my dad burst into my bedroom and pulled me out of bed. He was in a panic. He hurried my little sister and me into the backseat of our camper. My mother was in the front seat, gasping for air. Years later I would learn that my dad was praying desperately that night to spare my mother's life and take him instead. I laid there in a makeshift bed on the backseat, disoriented and afraid, as my dad sped down the highway while my mother sat suffocating.

We arrived at the hospital emergency room where my mother was immediately admitted. My sister and I never even got out of the camper.

In the morning, the three of us returned to visit her. However, my mother had slipped into a coma during the night and the hospital had strict policies against young children visiting with such patients. My dad pleaded with the staff, arguing that this might be the last time we would see our mother, but they would not relent. Instead, he visited her alone while my sister and I sat in the waiting room. The hospital seemed as cold and sterile as its policies.

Later that evening as we slept, my dad received a phone call from the hospital and was summoned back. He rushed over and entered my mother's room as they were trying to resuscitate her. Lying naked on the bed, her pale body jumped with a jolt of the paddles. My father stood watching, horrified. A nurse saw him and ushered him quickly out of the room. There was nothing more they could do. Hands shaking, my father signed the necessary hospital forms and returned home. It was December 26, 1977.

Early the next morning, my dad awakened me gently. I immediately sensed something was wrong. I got out of bed and followed him down the hall, which seemed to stretch on forever. My aunt and uncle were sitting in the living room, red-eyed. *Why are they here?* I wondered. My dad took me into my sister's room where he sat us both down on either side of him on the bed.

Then wrapping his arms around us, he said, "Girls, your mother died in the hospital last night."

A chilling heaviness gripped my heart. My father suddenly broke down crying, as did my little sister who was just six years old. But for reasons I didn't understand, I found myself putting my arms around my dad and repeating over and over, "It will be okay, Dad. It will be okay."

I was eight years old, and suddenly I was all grown up. From that moment, a sense of obligation began that would greatly affect the rest of my life. And Christmas would be altered, forever.

Chapter Three
Awakening

My mother's funeral was like a strange moving picture with haunting images of strangers dressed in black, stoic faces washed with tears, and an open casket I was not permitted to view.

"I don't want the last image of your mother to be her lifeless face lying in a casket," my dad told my little sister and me. I was being protected from something forbidden and mysterious. It was surreal.

At the graveside service, I sat in the front row with a long-stemmed rose in my hand and a hooded coat over my shoulders. Crowds of friends, family, and those who had played a part in my mother's short life gathered behind me in folding chairs. At the end of the service, her casket was lowered slowly into the earth. It was then that I realized she would not be coming back. Like my warm breath billowing out into the frozen air, my life ahead would be chillingly different without her. The cold morning mist enveloped me like her love once had and like the emptiness now did.

Over the following weeks, family and friends came to help us make the difficult transition. They cleaned and cooked and did laundry all day long. During the night, sounds of my father sobbing awakened me. It was the most horrible sound I had ever heard as he cried out into the darkness for my mother. I tried pulling the covers over my head to block it out, but there was no escaping it.

My grandmother, my father's mother, became my gentle caregiver during those weeks and months following my mother's death. She was a loving and attentive woman, nurturing me steadfastly with her kindness. In order to fall asleep at night, my grandmother tucked me in and then turned on a tape player at my bedside. Beautiful strains of *Silent Night, The First Noel,* and *Away in a Manger* played softly in my ears as I drifted off to unconsciousness every night. I wanted Christmas to never end, the final remnant of my mother's brief existence.

Shortly after her funeral, my mother's crafts and artwork disappeared from the shelves and walls of our home. Her beautiful creations were gone forever. Without a word, her perfumes and lotions and dresses all vanished. Her makeup and wig, painful reminders of her life, were gone, too. As a token gesture, I was given my mother's small jewelry box containing a few remaining jewelry pieces she had collected over the years. Everything else was given away, thrown away, or hidden away.

Our life was changing rapidly. My aunt came in once a week and cleaned my bedroom, and my grandmother continued to cook for me and do my laundry. We were surrounded by family and friends nearly all of the time. But one day, the three of us were home alone—my dad, my little sister, and me. For the first time in weeks, the house was quiet, and everyone had gone home for a few hours. We stood around the kitchen table opening mail. Then my dad paused for a moment with an envelope from the DMV. He opened it slowly and began to weep. Grabbing a chair, he fell into it as the papers dropped onto the table. My mother's new driver's license lay among them, her recent photo face-up. The photo was the last ever taken of her and was dated December 12, her birthday, just two weeks prior to her death. My dad was now sobbing uncontrollably, and soon we were all swept up in the grief.

There would be no more performing plays for my mother or warm angelic baths together. There would be no more early morning rituals or orange-spiced tea. There would be no more gardenia perfume or *Moonlight Sonata* on her clarinet. I didn't realize how final this goodbye would be. In fact, I was never actually able to say goodbye. She was just gone. At the age of thirty-two, she was gone. In a way, it may have been a blessing that I was too young to realize the full impact of what had just happened or to feel the tragic loss. I did sense one thing, however, and that was that I needed to be strong. There was work to do.

That summer we moved to Mission Viejo, a little community in Orange County closer to my dad's work as a junior high school music teacher. I became the woman of the house in many ways, learning to cook, to clean, to do laundry, and to care for my little sister. We were latch-key kids, waking up alone each morning, getting ourselves ready, and walking to the bus stop. Then we would come home to an empty house every day after school. I also took it upon myself to comfort my dad. As I grew more attached to him, I became a "daddy's girl," somewhat clingy for his attention and love. I needed him now more than ever.

Soon after we moved into our new home, my dad bought a piano—the first one we had ever owned—and he taught himself to play *Moonlight Sonata*. My sister and I sat beside him at the piano as he played the song over and over every night in the dim light of our living room. The haunting melody floated up to the ceiling where it seemed to linger like a ghost watching over us. Beethoven still looked on, as ominous as ever.

There were small things my father did to remind himself of my mother during this time. Things he did without saying a word and perhaps without even realizing it. The line between past and present seemed to blur as we became reminders ourselves of the quaint and happy life we had once lived. He was searching in his own way for answers, crossing the threshold of the past, while seeking for another world that held him spellbound in a way he couldn't quite understand. He returned to his childhood church where he began serious prayer and devotion. He began reading accounts of near-death experiences and speaking with extended family members about their own encounters with death. He was reaching out for a God who had eluded him his whole life—a God who was a foreign idea to us all. There had never been religion or spirituality in our home, and we didn't know what happened to those who passed on or if we would ever see my mother again. But somehow her memory seemed ever present, ever alive, as if she walked the halls of our home, hovering over our conversations and reaching out to us through my dad's quiet but persistent longings for her.

Lining the walkway that led to our front door was a beautiful new row of blooming gardenias, my mother's favorite flower, fragrant and alive, recently planted there by a man who had a foot in both worlds.

* * * * * * *

At school, I was shy and introverted. Gone was the flamboyant little girl at center stage. My imaginary spotlight had lost its luster, and I now wanted only to hide behind the curtains. Because of stress, I developed a pre-ulcerous condition and missed so much school that I nearly failed fourth grade. I didn't want the other students to know I wasn't like them.

For Mother's Day, I made a gift for my grandmother and labeled it "Mother." The other girls came to school with pretty French braids in their hair and trendy outfits their mothers had picked out for them. But I was an ugly girl with a tragic secret. When the day came for my fifth grade maturation program, a mother-daughter tea, my wise grandmother sent in a plate of cookies labeled "Mrs. Taylor." She never knew how much that small gesture meant to me.

At age eleven, I began keeping a journal, recording daily experiences and details from my life. My journal served as a friend to me, a trusted companion, and a source for expressing the things I could not say aloud.

> *July 28, 1980*
> *My sister had a big argument with Dad. Almost went to the movies. Stayed up late and watched television with Dad. Got up early to eat breakfast. My sister was crying because she was thinking about Dad dying. We had bad times.*

Adolescence came early for me. The summer following my mother's death, I started puberty, a terrifying ordeal without a mother to guide me through it. On the first day of sixth grade, I awoke in a puddle of blood. I had started my period sometime during the night. Since we didn't have feminine protection in the house, and I was too embarrassed to ask for it, I used toilet paper in my panties each month. Invariably blood leaked onto my clothes during the school day. I spent most of those days in the nurse's office. When I finally did start using feminine protection, I naively flushed it down the toilet the first time. As the drain clogged and water overflowed, I stood there, horrified, while my dad pulled my used pad out of the toilet with a hanger. I felt self-conscious and more awkward than ever.

Three years after my mother's death, I lay on my bed and cried. Not for the loneliness or the embarrassment or the humiliation of my awkward life now. These tears were for the sadness of my mother's death, and they were flowing for the first time. I cried for her suffering; I remembered it too well. I cried for the hair on her pillow and the blood in her sink, for her trembling hands and her big pink scar. I cried for her lost laughter and her yellow skin, for all of her beautiful things, reminders of her life long gone. I cried for her once sweet music, now silenced, and for our angelic baths together when her body was whole and perfect. I cried for the pain of Christmas, forever overshadowed. I cried for me, for my dad, for my little sister, and for our empty little house. I cried because I wanted her to return. I could vividly imagine a random knock at the door one day, and opening it to find her standing there on the porch, young and vibrant. I could see her face so clearly, her blue eyes and that glimmer she held in them. There had been some kind of mistake, and she was still alive, just missing for a while. I let myself feel it all—the loss, the hurt, the broken heart. I felt the finality of her absence.

And then I finally said goodbye.

* * * * * * *

In my sixth grade year, my dad began dating a woman with two teenage daughters. They met at the church we attended. During their dates, my little sister and I did small things to encourage them, such as setting out wine glasses with sparkling cider so they could enjoy a romantic evening together. We urgently wanted a mother and, notwithstanding our eagerness, it was our way of helping to make this happen. But as it turned out, our efforts were not needed. My dad fell fast, and he fell hard. After a brief series of dates and combined family activities, they became engaged and were married that summer. Visions of mother-daughter teas, shopping for bras, and French braids filled my head. I could hardly wait to start my new life.

My new stepmom, Isabel, and her two daughters moved into our house and we became a family. However, my dad immediately informed my little sister and me that he would be giving most of his attention and love to our new stepsisters. Their own father had been absent much of their lives growing up, he explained, and my dad felt they needed more love than we did. I took his word for it, but inside I felt like I was losing him. Perhaps he was just trying to be the best stepfather he could be. Nevertheless, I felt abandoned. We had grown immensely close during the three-and-a-half years together as a single-parent family. I had come to admire my dad for his selflessness and for his diligent and conscientious care of my sister and me. He had sacrificed greatly to give us what we needed. Though I was happy for him, it scared me to feel my dad slipping away from me.

I hoped that having a mother again would fill in the empty space, but soon after they were married it was discovered that Isabel had a chemical imbalance and severe bi-polar depression. She had angry and frightening episodes on a regular basis, after which she would retreat to her bedroom and hibernate for days on end. Though she was typically a lovely and outgoing person, these emotional episodes made it extremely difficult for me to accept her. Our household often felt like a landmine. We had to be cautious of everything we said or did for risk of triggering her.

One day, I approached my dad about my feelings.

"She's sick and can't help herself," he told me. "Isabel has an illness, like Carol had. You need to be more patient and understanding."

This is nothing like what my mother had, I thought. She had suffered a terrible disease while chemotherapy ravaged her body. But my stepmom screamed till her face turned bright red, yelling angry words and often breaking things.

My father's words stung.

My sister and I were not allowed to speak of my mother for fear of hurting our stepmom's feelings. Our mother was now referred to as "Carol." We had a new "mother" now. Even my mother's jewelry box that I had inherited had to be hidden away. Shortly after, I inadvertently discovered a nude photograph of her tucked secretly in the bottom compartment of the jewelry box. She was lying in an alluring pose and looked to be in her early twenties. Here was something new of my mother, something intimate and beautiful, unlike anything I had ever seen. In my excitement, I showed the photo to my dad, who promptly confiscated it.

"If Isabel ever saw this, she would be very upset," he told me.

I never saw the photo again.

I felt as if my mother had died twice—first, in body that tragic night in December 1977, and second, in spirit, as her belongings disappeared and I was no longer allowed to speak of her. It was as though she was vanishing from existence. I longed for my mother and for the memory of her life, which now seemed distant and almost forgotten. I wanted her to hold me close and tell me a story like she had done so many times. Her extraordinary imagination had always transported me someplace magical, drawing me into a world of wonder with her words. Through mystical tunnels and to enchanted hillsides, spellbinding characters came to life, and little girls lived happily ever after. I wanted her to take me there now—to a place where anything was possible. I wanted to feel her breath on my face and know that she was still there somewhere. Though I did not know if my mother still existed, I began reaching out to her in my thoughts, exploring the idea that she was alive somehow, and secretly communicating to her.

My little sister and I both struggled to adapt to our shifting world. During our pre-teen years, she became distant, troubled, and rebellious. Her volatile behavior escalated, often erupting in angry confrontations. Our relationship became strained. Because she and I had always been close, I was admonished by my dad to be a good example to her. But I felt ill prepared to be her role model or to take on any responsibility for her actions. We were both dealing with the dramatic life-changes in our own different ways, just trying to make sense of the new life being handed to us.

With the new union of our two families, my parents adopted a very strict family standard. They chose to raise us under a stiff moral code of tight curfews, restrictive dating standards, and stringent expectations that we were required to live up to with no exceptions. This was a very different landscape from the casual and nurturing environment I was used to. In their endeavor to raise the "perfect" family, my parents implemented regular family counsels and personal accountability. They laid a foundation of spiritual values and character-driven virtues for us to follow. They also taught us principles such as integrity, faith, and commitment. But the contrast between the tight standards of perfection and the lack of nurturing left me feeling confused, unappreciated, and never quite good enough. Despite the value of these idealistic standards, all I wanted at the time was for someone to put their arms around me and accept me for who I was. I wanted to feel loved, regardless of my imperfections.

This new lifestyle was born of the higher path on which my dad now found himself. With Isabel, he discovered the spirituality he had longingly sought after my mother's death. It was cemented in the religious devotion they both shared, and in the devotion we, as a family, now embraced.

My dad had become more introspective, and there was a distinct sense of reverence about him now that had not been there before. He still went to work every day, served his family, and played music, but he had changed somehow. And though I didn't fully understand it, I sensed in him a newfound wisdom. Isabel, too, was becoming someone different as she sought ways to soften the hardship of my mother's death.

"I will never try and replace your real mother," she once confided in me, "but I will always love you, LeeAnn."

* * * * * * *

In high school, I grew out of my awkwardness and became very independent—a quality my mother had instilled in me as a young girl. School afforded me the opportunity for expression and freedom I could not have at home. It was also an escape from the turmoil I felt from my sister's rebellion and my stepmother's bi-polar depression.

During my freshman year, I found my niche in choir and drama, where I excelled rapidly. I loved being in the center of creativity. It was a nexus of fascination, and I became happier than I had been in years. I felt drawn to the performing arts as my life's work and was finally recapturing the magic of my childhood dreams.

During this time, I also began writing poetry and exploring other forms of artistic self-expression. I was unconventional and eccentric, both in my dress and in my outlook. I was a young woman who celebrated one-of-a-kindness with flair. Neon tights and patent leather boots coupled with spiked blonde hair and lacy petticoats became my trademark. My long hair-pieces and off-the-shoulder wraps added a feminine glamour to the punk style I had adopted, reflecting a confident young woman who was not only emerging, but also exploring her individuality and pushing the boundaries. Love for beautiful things such as art and music flourished within me, and a new appreciation for personal fulfillment took hold.

At school, I became a fascinated observer, watching the people around me—the students and faculty who walked beside me on campus. I wondered if they saw the magic in life the way I now did. At home, I was busy mapping out my life's path and career aspirations. I decided I was a non conformist and would march to the beat of my own drum, regardless of what others thought of me. I knew I was different, and I fell in love with the idea of being an original. I also had all the attention I wanted for my beauty and flamboyant self-expression. This, too, defined and invigorated me.

It was during my junior year that I began to grow spiritually. As I pondered and observed and questioned the world around me, I felt my perspective begin to shift. I began to view life and its experiences more deeply. I believed there was more than just the superficial social structure of the high school scene. There seemed to be an unseen world, which pulsated and flowed through me, something bigger which elevated me in those quiet moments alone. I also knew that I was different, that there was something about me that didn't fit, beyond the neon tights and leather fringe. I began to feel, at times, like an outsider living on the inside, and I wondered if anyone would understand what was happening to me.

> *January 5, 1986*
> *Well, a new year has come, and a lot of things have changed. I've changed. I see life in a different light. I'm growing both mentally and spiritually. I know I have a great mission to accomplish during my life. I am excited about life and I want to go as far as I possibly can. I know I can be successful. I know I can go far . . .*

My prayers became more sincere and intimate during this time. I felt there was someone truly listening. I also sensed my mother was somehow aware of me, somehow present, even though I could neither see nor touch her. I became very introspective as I tapped into this heightened understanding, which I felt existed in an unseen universe. I sought divinity within myself, and spiritual gifts began to emerge. I found I had the ability to discern the nature of a person's character without having known them, as if reading their inner motives. I also had the ability to grasp deep spiritual concepts with ease, almost like *remembering* them. I experienced a kind of private renaissance—an awakening—and I truly came into my own. My spirituality blossomed and flourished, touching every part of my world. I felt closer to a higher power, a being who was moving upon my heart in powerful and unexpected ways, and inspiration flowed freely into my life.

> *March 17, 1986*
> *My life has changed so greatly. I want to sing to the world the great love I am feeling in my heart, in my soul. I am so blessed—more than I can ever express by the tip of my pen. Something very incredible is happening in my life. What a light I have discovered in myself.*

Then, while sleeping on the night of December 9, 1986, I found myself in the midst of a bright and gentle light. The pervasive brightness that surrounded me had substance to it, as if particles of luminous energy suffused the air around me. Though I was asleep, I was fully lucid. And I soon realized I was outside of my body in a place of profound calm.

About one foot away and facing me, I beheld a young woman. Her face was flawless and beautiful, reminiscent of a delicate china doll, with a deep luminosity that originated far beneath the surface. Light emanated from her, framing her face in a manner similar to a frosted silhouette one might see in an oval photograph, dissolving around the edges into the whiteness. Her hair was long and pulled back, and she appeared to be about twenty years old, though there was a distinct agelessness to her.

I was mesmerized by how much this girl looked like me—a reflection of me somehow—a mirror image almost. We faced each other for a long moment before I finally recognized her. Though it wasn't so much a recognition as it was a *realization* of who she was. The last time I had seen her she was pale and sick and bald, unlike the radiant perfect young woman before me now—a timeless angel encased in light.

It was Carol, my mother. I was in her heavenly presence, and she had a message for me.

She immediately began expressing her love for me and her joy for my self-discovery and newfound spirituality. This love washed over me fully, infusing me from head-to-toe with its encompassing power. Unlike an exchange of words, these were feelings and concepts communicated directly to my spirit, instantaneous and all-expansive. With an ability that came instinctively to me, I simultaneously shared my joy and longing for her in this same manner—directly to her spirit. Mere words could never have accomplished such a sweeping expression. Also radiating through me was a deep certainty that God existed, that He loved me, and was elated for my progress. All of this was given as though my entire body was a conduit of love. Multiple layers of meanings and understandings were overlapping in a graceful flow of sacred expression, and it truly swept through my entire being, completely redefining for me what love is.

I allowed myself to be absorbed into it, to feel with every cell in me the substance of my mother's spirit, the power of her presence. There was no thought of my life before this moment or what would happen after. There was only love flowing into me, through me, and around me, penetrating every fiber and completely embracing me in its fullness. I wanted to remain here with her forever.

At the same time, I was able to perceive the experience from above and from the sides, moving around my mother and me in a panoramic view that revealed every detail of our encounter in perfect clarity. At first, I didn't understand how it was possible for me to see with such scope. However, I was given to understand that the eyes of our spirit see all dimensions from every angle simultaneously.

My mother then looked deeply into my eyes, drawing me in, locking me in her penetrating gaze. She held me there firmly for a long, spellbinding moment. And then I saw it—that same glimmer that had been there when I was a young girl, the same spark that spoke volumes from her eyes before the cancer snuffed it out. It took hold of me, piercing me to the very core.

After nine long years, my mother and I were one again.

We were one.

She then expressed a specific word to my soul, *"Farewell."*

I immediately awoke.

I sat up in bed, overcome by the penetrating love that still lingered. Tears began falling. I had been someplace else, in an otherworldly realm of love and light. I had seen my mother—she had actually communicated with me. It was not only a confirmation of the spiritual direction my life had taken, but I now knew that she still loved me, that she was proud of me. And more importantly, somewhere, in some distant beautiful place, my mother still *lived*.

This unique and profound experience would cast a mystical halo over my life. And though I remained bound to the mortal world, her supernal presence would never leave me.

I continued to explore my spirituality during this time, drawing nearer to a divine source. I seldom let anyone see this side of me; it was too personal, too private. After the experience with my mother, I knew there was more than what the visible eye could behold. I felt constantly drawn to this spiritual pull as a mysterious part of me yearned to be fully realized. I allowed myself to grow with it, to be embraced by it, to feel its sublime yet compelling surge as it took hold of me. This spirituality wasn't the product of my parents' religious standards or my family's imposed model of perfection, but rather a result of my own searching, my own longing, born in the quiet crevasses of my own heart. I held it close, clinging to its light and empowered by its peace. And in those moments, I found higher hope than what the world had ever offered me.

* * * * * * *

I finished high school, receiving top honors in performing arts and the award for best actress two years in a row. My course was set; my direction clear. I would be an actress and would set the world ablaze, powered by the confidence held in my newfound spirituality and motivated by a lifetime of dreams. That young, idealistic girl still held in her mind's eye the vision of success and hope. She set her sights on something larger than life, and with her naïve ambition she reached out and caught hold of an idea that she would take the world by storm.

After graduation, I entered a training program in film acting and began modeling in fashion and hair shows. I was cast as a face character in various parades at Disneyland with expressive individuals like myself. My parents were surprisingly supportive of my decision to go into the entertainment industry and were helping me chart a successful course ahead. They had relaxed on their stringent expectations, and they now treated me like a respected adult.

I loved my life and the opportunities coming to me. I planned to become well established in my career before thinking about marriage. I was only nineteen, after all. I could get married later—much later—after I was thirty or so. Maybe I would even have two or three children eventually. But that was a million miles away. There was so much life to live, and I was going to live it fully.

The world would know who LeeAnn Taylor was.

My little sister and I were on relatively decent terms, though our relationship had been somewhat strained. One day, she suggested I join her on a double date with her boyfriend and his best friend, someone I hadn't seen since I was fourteen years old. His name was Kyle.

Chapter Four

A New Horizon

At fourteen years old, I went to church youth dances nearly every weekend, jumping to the pounding music and neon lights and staying out on the dance floor for every song. It was at one of these dances where I met Kyle for the first time, an eighteen-year-old blond-haired, blue-eyed prep. As he held me in his arms during one particular slow dance, a warmth covered me from head to toe, and a sweet calmness filled me, leaving me with a tingle long after the song was over. When the night ended, we met up frequently at social gatherings and dances. Though I was decidedly boy-crazy at the time, something about Kyle was different. He surprised me by leaving colorful notes and homemade cards on my doorstep—silly things no one had ever done for me. We became quickly enamored with each other, but because I was only fourteen at the time, my parents informed me that I was too young to date. Kyle and I broke off our relationship, and we lost contact for five years.

I was a little skeptical of seeing him after all this time. But when my sister and I pulled into the parking lot to meet our dates for the drive-in movie, I instantly recognized Kyle's endearing smile and gentle eyes. He was more confident, yet still soft spoken and respectful, and I was impressed. A few days later, we went on another date and there was a spark of something unique between us. As we walked hand-in-hand that night, I felt a sort of glow, similar to our first meeting on the dance floor five years prior. I loved the way he treated me. He was kind and attentive, and thoughtfully accommodating. As we sat in the cab of his small pick-up truck during the end of our second date, we talked until the early morning hours about our dreams and ambitions. I even let him see my spiritual side, something I allowed very few people to see.

Things progressed quickly, even mysteriously, and we found ourselves talking of things we had each decided we would only discuss with our future spouses. On our fifth date, just two weeks after the drive-in movie, we stood outside my house and shared our first kiss. He had just asked me to marry him.

And I said, "Yes."

Kyle and I knew we were meant to be together. It was a crazy kind of wonderful; an unexpected tidal wave that swept over us, blindsiding us both with all the force and power of true love. Neither of us had planned a serious relationship, but the strong impressions and the way it was unfolding made it undeniable. It was as if there was some force drawing us together.

This came as a surprise to both of our families. My two stepsisters had married that same year, and my parents were still recovering financially. They were shocked to hear that I was engaged so quickly, but were unexpectedly supportive. In fact, there seemed to be an air of excitement among all of us that this was an important union, an inspired union, perhaps even a kind of miracle.

> *July 23, 1988*
> *We've been together every day for the past three weeks. I still can't believe how happy Kyle and I are. Every minute with him is so wonderful. We are just crazy in love! I can't wait till we get married. Kyle and I are meant to be.*

This new path felt so exhilarating. All of my previous notions of waiting until I was thirty to get married simply melted away at the idea of being with Kyle. We were in the prime of our youth and ready to take on the world. We spent every day together, every moment possible, planning and preparing for our amazing new life together.

Our courtship had been dramatically short and there was still so much to learn about each other. I told Kyle of my desire to wait to have children. I was getting married years sooner than I had originally planned, and I wasn't ready to start a family yet. I was just nineteen and Kyle was almost twenty-three. We discussed having two or three children eventually, but we agreed we would wait at least five years. I didn't want a big family; nor did I dream of being a mother, at least not since I was a little girl with a baby doll—not since my mother died.

In our discussions, Kyle and I were both in favor of less-traditional roles in marriage. I expressed my desire for a career, and he gave me his full support. He promised he would never impose a traditional role on me. He encouraged me in my career ambitions, and I supported him in his dream of becoming an entrepreneur. He had already started a small business and had hopes of one day owning several large corporations. I saw greatness in him, and believed he could do anything.

Kyle was the youngest of six children and was openly referred to as his mother's favorite. He was often the center of attention in his family and was still partially supported by his parents. His mother was unquestionably the head of their household, and she made it clear to me in her own way that nobody was good enough for her son. She was especially displeased when she learned of our plans to wait to have children. She openly opposed it.

It would be a relief to finally be out on our own and building our ideal future. Kyle and I supported each other's passions and dreams and were elated to be embarking on this grand adventure together. From where we stood, our future looked spectacular. I had found true love, something many people search their entire lives for and never find. I felt immensely fortunate, deeply happy, and for the first time in my life, truly independent.

One night, shortly before our wedding, Kyle and I stood outside my house and held each other in the moonlight. Neither of us spoke a word. His breath on my cheek warmed me, sending chills up and down my spine.

He gave a tender squeeze around my waist every few minutes to remind me how much I was loved. The air was calm and the sky was dark and clear. Stars hovered above like glimmering spectators silently cheering us on. It seemed we could stand in that silent embrace forever, just the two of us in the intimate stillness, like no one else on the planet existed. Somehow I knew that all was right in the universe.

* * * * * * *

Kyle and I were married on December 9, 1988, in a modest ceremony in Los Angeles, just five months after our first date and exactly two years since the mystical encounter with my mother's spirit. It all felt very significant, as if the heavens were shining on us, bright with the promise of a happy and successful life ahead.

Our honeymoon in San Francisco lasted only three days. After two traffic tickets, our car being towed, and spending our last hundred dollars at the impound yard, our promising life together started out as a hellacious nightmare. Out of money and emotionally defeated, we returned home early.

Once back, we rented a one-bedroom apartment in Mission Viejo, California, where I grew up. Mission Viejo was quintessential suburbia, with beautiful green hills and cookie-cutter houses overlooking the distant brown smog of Los Angeles. It was home to wealthy young families and executive couples eagerly working their way up the ladder of success. It had status written all over it—the kind of place that would be a perfect backdrop for our lofty aspirations. We both worked minimum wage jobs, and I continued to train for an acting career. Kyle had taken a few community college classes, but he decided to put off school. We established ourselves in a local branch of our church and began building a new social life. Though our lifestyle was a bit beyond our humble means, we were confident that financial prosperity was just over the horizon.

Two weeks after our December wedding, we enjoyed our first Christmas together. It was a marathon of presents. We had saved all of our wedding gifts in addition to the Christmas gifts we had bought for each other. There we sat in our flannel pajamas, wide-eyed and giddy on our apartment floor Christmas morning in a sea of gift-wrapped treasures. We opened one brightly wrapped package after another. Crystal vases, porcelain dishes, toasters, wine glasses, and mounds upon mounds of towels filled our apartment. In the corner of the room stood a twelve-foot Douglas fir decorated with paper wedding bells and topped with a red and white Christmas bear. It was Rockwell-picturesque.

I was a woman now; it was official. Even though I was only nineteen years old, I felt like an adult with real adult responsibilities—a marriage, my own home, my own life. I was making my own way in the world. I pondered my mother at my age, newly married with her whole life ahead of her.

I wonder what it was like for you, Mom.

I tried not to think about her early death, but it was nearly impossible not to during December. The Christmas season seemed to be the depository for every memory of my mother.

I hope you were truly fulfilled.

Life would be my chance to redeem her loss, a starting point for a joyful and fulfilling experience for us both. I allowed hope to carry me forward into its waiting arms.

Together, Kyle and I were a powerhouse. Strangers approached us in the grocery store or at the gas station and remarked how striking we were together. We felt we had the support of the universe for our success. We set ambitious one-, three-, five-, and ten-year goals. We planned for Kyle's successful business ventures as an entrepreneur; he was going to be a millionaire by the time he was thirty. We planned for my prolific career as a famous movie star. We planned for a huge custom home, new cars, and abundant wealth.

And we put children on the five-year page.

February 23, 1989
Kyle and I have been married for two and a half months. We have been
so happy. At 9:30 pm tonight, the home pregnancy test proved positive! I
can't believe I'm pregnant!

CHAPTER FIVE
The Light Expands

I was devastated.

Kyle and I were fairly naïve about birth control. We had both been raised in conservative, religious families. The topic of sexuality had been virtually unmentioned in our childhood homes, and we had never been intimate with anyone else. When I received my physical exam prior to obtaining a marriage license, the nurse told me I didn't need to use birth control; she assured me that my body's natural rhythms would be sufficient. In addition, I had been warned by my doctor to avoid the birth control pill because of my high risk for breast cancer. Though I took this risk very seriously, that decision would later prove dangerous in its own right.

As with all the other challenging situations I had met with in my life, I committed to making the best of this unexpected pregnancy. I was an idealist, an eternal optimist, and this situation demanded every ounce of positivity I could give it. That Friday, we called our parents and told them the news of the pregnancy. The following Tuesday, I left work early and went home to rest; I had begun spotting. By the afternoon, I was writhing in pain and bleeding heavily. I didn't understand what was happening to me. My obstetrician was on vacation, and I didn't know who else to call.

Because we had only one car at the time, I was scheduled to pick up Kyle from work, a forty-five minute drive. I called him and begged him to get a ride home. I was in too much pain, and didn't think I could make the trip. But he insisted I come get him. Though I was in extreme pain, neither of us realized the seriousness of the situation.

"Please call a cab," I asked again, "I can barely move."

But he was firm, "You need to come get me."

I reluctantly pulled myself out of bed and managed to get to the car. The drive was excruciating and I cried the whole way back.

Once home, I went straight to the bathroom while Kyle tried to contact a doctor who could help us. He made call after call, but no one would help. I was doubled over now and bleeding profusely. Moments later, I screamed in horror. I had just passed two large clots. Kyle came running into the bathroom, but neither of us knew what to do. We rushed to the hospital where I was taken to emergency admissions.

As I stared up at the white ceiling tiles, nurses and doctors worked busily to prepare me for emergency surgery.

"How long have you kids been married?" one of the nurses asked.

"Two months," I answered, feigning bravery to conceal the trembling which had started through my body.

My clothes were removed and IV's were hooked into my arm. A strange metal contraption was inserted between my legs to remove blood and tissue samples.

"You wouldn't have wanted this pregnancy to continue," said the doctor-on-call. I began crying.

"Count backwards from one hundred, LeeAnn."

Kyle held my hand as the chemicals surged into my bloodstream with a chill, running icy waves through my veins. Strangers rushed around me while the cold, sterile room went black.

"Ninety-nine . . . ninety-eight . . . ninety-seven . . ."

* * * * * *

Hours later, I awoke in a post-surgery room. I looked around, disoriented and groggy from the anesthesia. Then I noticed an orange dye coating my thighs and lower abdomen. They had scraped out my uterus while I slept. The baby was gone.

For the next several hours, I lay in a hospital bed while Kyle and my parents stood close by. I felt nauseated, in pain, and so vulnerable. When early morning came, Kyle and I returned home. Even though the pregnancy had been an unwelcomed surprise, I felt a deep sense of sadness in its loss. I walked into our bedroom and began clearing off the bed so I could lie down. I just wanted to forget the events of the last twenty-four hours.

Kyle picked up a piece of folded paper from my nightstand and began opening it.

"It's nothing," I said, quickly grabbing it from him and hoping he didn't notice the tears forming in my eyes.

"Let me see," he said and gently took the paper.

Inside was a list of baby names I had scribbled down just days earlier. We stood there, silent, looking at the list. He placed the paper back on the nightstand and wrapped his arms around me. There was nothing more to say.

I spent the next few days in bed recovering. Immediately—and to my horror—I began receiving condolence calls from people I didn't even know. *Who could have known about this pregnancy?* I wondered. I had only known about it for four days myself. But the news of my pregnancy had spread quickly through Kyle's family, and so had the news of my miscarriage. I felt my privacy had been violated, and I resented the fact that I now had to speak courteously over the phone about something very personal and painful to me. Even though they were well-meaning people, I began to feel uncomfortable with Kyle's family. It was clear that I was different, that I was not who his mother would have chosen for him. He was held in such high regard, it made me feel like a second-class citizen.

After the miscarriage, we discovered the cost wasn't covered under our insurance. This imposed a financial strain on us. We were barely making ends meet. But I had warmed to the idea of having a baby. I felt that perhaps we could wait a few months and then possibly start a family. Our medical bills would be paid off by then and we would be in a better position financially. I believed that with Kyle's support, I could still build my career and manage a baby at the same time.

We enjoyed the following months as newlyweds. However, our intimate life was not what I expected it would be. Due to our inexperience, there was so much neither of us knew. Sexual ignorance can be a very dangerous thing. Because I hadn't had an orgasm yet, we assumed I must be sexually dysfunctional. Kyle suggested I see a therapist to get help, but I was too humiliated and ashamed. I couldn't accept the possibility that there might be something wrong with me. We had been so affectionate before the wedding, but within the first few weeks of our marriage, all foreplay stopped abruptly. The entire sexual experience lasted less than two minutes, and I thought this was normal.

Maybe it was being raised in a home where sexual discussions were taboo, or maybe it was our inexperience. But since I didn't know any better and was too embarrassed to ask for help, I actually bought into the idea that I had a problem.

This false assumption would plague our entire marriage.

* * * * * *

In the spring, I was given a very special gift from my father. The collection of scrapbooks, photo albums, and yearbooks belonging to my mother was finally handed over to me. I would now have the privilege of reading about her, digging through her keepsakes, and seeing her life laid out before me. Little details like love letters, personal notes, and old photographs captioned with her own handwriting awaited me. There were even original songs she had composed. I was so thrilled to begin looking through her life, I could hardly wait. I put the entire collection in the backseat of our car for the long hours I would have each afternoon.

We still shared one car, so Kyle dropped me off at work every morning and then drove to his job thirty miles away. On his lunch break, he had just enough time to come get me and bring me back to his work where I waited until he was finished for the day, usually about three hours. The forty-five minute drive both ways made the cost of gas a big expense for two kids working minimum-wage jobs, so I often opted to sit in the car and wait until he was done. Besides, this would afford me the perfect opportunity to go through my mother's keepsakes undistracted, where I could lay out every book and savor each page. I felt drawn to get to know this woman, to search any remnants of her life, to see who she was and what we shared in common. The mystical encounter with her was still fresh in my mind, leaving me with a longing to bring her somehow nearer.

The first afternoon was a hot one with the California sun beating down on the windows of our small compact car. The vinyl seats seemed to trap the heat and made my legs stick. I laid a towel down and worked to get comfortable in the back seat. It allowed the most room for spreading out the books and albums.

I started with my mother's childhood scrapbook, a delicate paper album with brown pages that crumbled and crackled around the edges. The book opened with old-fashioned cards and announcements celebrating her birth. It was the close of 1945 and World War II had just ended. The tiny cards were embellished with pink and blue paintings of a perfect baby wrapped in a ruffled cradle, indicative of a prosperous new era in America. There were many congratulations from family, friends, and loved ones—most of whom I had never heard of. It was evident my mother's birth was a very special event in her family.

The following pages included elementary school report cards, progress reports, and birthday cards. Photos of a freckle-faced little girl with ribbons in her hair made me smile. I turned the pages to find teenaged pictures of my mother in a school band uniform. There were newspaper clippings featuring her playing the saxophone, and an article announcing her as the winner of the 1963 Music Scholarship Award. The article described her plans to one day become a music teacher and reported that she would be playing *Mozart's Concerto in A Minor* that evening.

On the next pages I found photographs of formal dances my mother attended. She was bright and bubbly, and had her arm linked to a different young man in every photo. There were proms, winter formals, Sadie Hawkins, and military balls, and she wore a different gown in each one. She was vivacious, yet elegant, with a slender neckline and alabaster skin. Her soft brown hair was meticulously coifed, and she still had a spattering of freckles across the bridge of her nose.

There was a light in my mother's eyes that sparkled in each photograph, a radiance that popped. This young woman was coming alive on the pages, breathing in and out of each photograph, each newspaper clipping. She was popular and engaging with a vibrancy that shouted off each page in big, bold letters. I took a deep breath and felt her spirit's energy flowing through the windows of our small car, blowing across my face like a whisper from the dust. She wanted me to find her, to know her, there in those pictures and music programs and newspaper clippings. She wanted me to see that she was still very much alive.

A few days passed until I was able to get back to the albums. With a cooler, cloudy sky overhead, I settled in with my towel on the back seat and picked up where I had left off the last time. My mother had just graduated high school and was a music major at Long Beach State College. Envelope after envelope of love letters from my father stationed in the Air National Guard lined the following pages. Carefully I opened one and began to read:

Dearest Carol,

I love you. I miss you. I wish I could be with you right now. I'd love to have my arms around you. You make life worthwhile for me. I hope you always love me.

All my love,
Lemoyne

They had just met in college and were already in love. My mother had made an enormous Valentine's Day card for him with a big red heart and the words *Be My Valentine, Mony Dear* on the front. I chuckled to myself about how soon after high school she had gotten engaged.

We are so alike, Mom.

After the love letters, there was a marriage license dated August 15, 1964. Photographs from my parents' first few years together covered the next several pages. In one photo, my mother had put on a few pounds and her hair was long—the only time she ever wore it that way. There were pictures of me on my first birthday, in my mother's arms standing in front of a new house. There were letters of recommendation for her teaching applications, and class pictures with her first group of students.

Then I turned the page to find a school faculty picture of my mother, taken just before she was diagnosed with cancer. That face I knew; that face I remembered. But something was different. She wore a labored smile, and there was a distant look in her eyes. A sudden chill ran up my spine. That light that shone in her eyes as a teenager—that vibrant spark—was missing. I turned the page and saw another picture with the same expression, and another one. Empty smiles and empty eyes.

Homemade get well cards from her students and faculty members followed:

Mrs. Taylor,
We hope you get well soon for all of us, because we miss you very much.
We want you to come back as soon as you can.

I closed the book and sat there quietly. I couldn't read any more letters or homemade cards or handwritten notes. And I couldn't look at any more photos—not those ones. I carefully organized the albums in a stack on the floor in the back seat and covered them with the towel. And then I waited, hoping Kyle wouldn't ask me about what I'd seen.

* * * * * * *

Summer arrived, and with it came a new development: I was pregnant. We were ready with a new doctor and a new insurance plan. The first five months of my pregnancy I was as sick as a dog. Between the vomiting and the insomnia, there seemed to be no relief. When I finally regained my appetite, all I wanted to eat was Chinese food and mint-chocolate-chip ice cream.

November 14, 1989
I first felt the baby kick at five months. We both think it's going to be a girl. The baby is due February 12, but I hope it will come sooner. Kyle and I have been able to hear the heartbeat. It's weird to think that I have a living person inside me. We also went for an ultrasound a few months ago and were able to actually see the baby. That was amazing. I hope it is a healthy baby.

My body was changing in all kinds of strange ways. I had always been very thin, but now I was packing on the weight. At nearly one-hundred-and-sixty pounds, I was a far cry from my former size-five, one-hundred-and-ten-pound figure. My feet were swollen, my face was swollen, and my belly was swollen. This was an adventure of a whole different kind.

I imagined the things my mother and I would have talked about if she were alive and how we would have laughed at my expanding profile.

What would you tell me right now, Mom? What should I know about motherhood? And will you be with me when my baby is born?

As sure as my heart could hope, my mother's spirit was walking with me through this experience, reaching out to hold my hand during this pivotal time.

I continued with my acting classes, training in the evenings twice a week. They were a wonderful creative outlet for me. My coach expressed concern that I wouldn't be able to keep up after the baby was born, but I assured him that I had plenty of support at home and could handle anything. Though I was excited for the new baby we would soon have, I didn't realize how fast my life was changing.

Kyle quit his minimum-wage job so he could take advantage of an opportunity to work with his oldest brother as a construction superintendent. The increased income enabled us to move into a two-bedroom apartment where I began preparations for our new arrival. We both had the distinct impression that our new baby would be a girl. With this in mind, I painted the baby furniture the same cheerful yellow of my childhood bedroom. In some way, it brought to life the expectations I harbored about the blissful experience I believed motherhood would be, and it kept in place the ideal which was ever present in my heart. I spent weeks creating a handmade baby book with original artwork and detailed notes about the pregnancy. I listened to classical music all day in hopes my baby would be smart. And I watched *I Love Lucy* and laughed a lot.

I wanted everything to be perfect.

February 1, 1990
Well, only two weeks left. I can't believe it's already here. I've been having a
lot of false contractions. I hope the baby comes soon. We've been attending
classes at the hospital for five weeks now. Tonight is our last class. I'm not
as scared to have the baby as I used to be. I'm just anxious now. It seems
like I've been pregnant forever.

I read several maternity books during the final months of my pregnancy. I wanted to be fully prepared. Kyle seemed to have a natural assurance about his fathering skills and was eagerly awaiting our new baby with calm and confidence. I wanted to be a good mother, and I felt that I had a lot of love to give. I also had specific ideas on how I wanted to raise this child. I would imbue her with my fiery determination and my grand ambition. I would teach her to dream big and then instill in her the self-confidence needed to achieve big dreams. I would tell her stories about brave little girls with stars in their eyes and then help her see how smart and beautiful she was. I would take long baths with her, holding her in my arms where she could peer into my eyes and see the love held in their glimmer. I promised I would tell her I loved her every day, and then I would show her in a thousand different ways so that she would never doubt it.

On the night of February 4, my water broke. The baby was coming seven days early. I woke up Kyle, and we made a mad dash for the hospital. Once there, I was set up in a maternity room. The nurse who tended to me was so impressed with how young and happy we were, we ended up talking with her about our ambitious life plans. The labor went smoothly, and after eight hours we had a tiny five-pound, red-haired girl in our arms. She was perfectly healthy and unusually alert. She opened her eyes immediately to take in her surroundings, as if she couldn't wait to get familiar with her new stomping ground.

February 8, 1990
Guess what? I had the baby on February 5! We had a beautiful baby
girl. Her name is Jaede. She has strawberry hair and blue eyes. She is just
beautiful! We love her so much. Kyle is so good with her. He is just crazy
about her. I'll keep you updated!

Friends and family brought in meals to us for the first few days after returning home. Though it took a while for life to settle into a routine, it didn't take long for us to get the hang of the parenting thing. Kyle was beaming with all the glow of a brand new dad and was amazingly natural with our new daughter. Jaede was precious, and motherhood was more amazing than I ever dreamed possible. Looking at this beautiful creation was awe-inspiring, and a great love came into my heart for the miraculous experience. I hadn't realized up to that point in my life what deep devotion I was capable of feeling. It was magical. I hardly slept the first few weeks, and it wasn't just because of midnight feedings. I simply wanted to watch my new daughter every second, to lean over her bassinet throughout the night and marvel at her delicate body and flawless skin. I didn't want to miss a thing. I wanted to record in my heart the wonder and majesty of this tiny angelic being.

I was a mother now. And it was larger than life.

Chapter Six
Love Is Other-Worldly

"I'm seeing some great work from you, LeeAnn. Keep it up," my acting coach said to me one night on my way out of class.

Motherhood had given me a surge of emotional depth, and I noticed a whole new quality in my dramatic work. I was more sensitive now, more perceptive, and more confident. I excelled in my advanced group and worked to lose the pregnancy weight so I could start auditioning for jobs.

I was breastfeeding Jaede at the time, but she refused to take a bottle while I was away at my class. Kyle walked with her almost continuously while she screamed at the top of her lungs. Afterwards, I rushed home to feed her as Kyle recounted for me the nightmare of trying to comfort a screaming baby for three hours. It ultimately became too frustrating and, just two months after Jaede was born, I quit my class. I didn't know when I would return. Caring for Jaede was a full-time job, and the obligation of being her only source of nourishment began to stress me. At four months old, I weaned her. This afforded me a little more freedom with my time.

Then I made a shocking discovery: I was pregnant again.

Kyle was excited. I was horrified. Our sole form of birth control was proving to be grossly insufficient. All it took was negligence one time in the heat of the moment. The thought of having another baby was overwhelming, and there was no way I could return to my class. I had to adapt. My sense of obligation took over, and I began to foster a positive attitude about this unexpected pregnancy. I reasoned that if I had both of my children close together, I would be able to pursue my career more fully afterwards.

Jaede and I only had a few months to bond before the new baby came, and I took full advantage of it. In the early morning hours when she awoke, I brought her into bed with me, wrapped her in a blanket, and laid her on my chest. The sound of my heartbeat lulled her to sleep and for hours we laid cuddled up together. During the day, I sang her lullabies and read her stories. She was very curious and exploratory and she developed ahead of her age, crawling and walking early.

November 4, 1990
It's been a long time since I've written to you. Jaede is already nine months old! She is so fun and cute! She has bright red hair and blue eyes. Guess what? We're expecting another baby. I'm already four months along! The baby is tentatively due on April 29. I think it might be a boy, but it's still too early to tell.

Kyle received a raise at work and we put a small deposit down on a condominium. The property was a two bedroom, one bath, upper-unit condo in Mission Viejo with a balcony and a one-car garage. It was only three years old and just over a thousand square feet. It was small, but nice, and we figured we would live there for a few years before moving into some place bigger once we were more established. We immediately moved into a bedroom in my parents' home in order to save for the down payment. We also sold our car and financed a small, used four-door sedan.

By the time I was six months pregnant, however, the stress of taking care of Jaede and Kyle in our little bedroom became stifling. Every time Jaede woke up during the night, I worried about waking my parents. Even though Isabel's depression had mellowed after I moved out and her angry episodes seemed to have ebbed, I still felt cautious about triggering her. I also felt pressured to act like our marriage was perfect. Kyle had become somewhat insensitive towards me at times and we were both under pressure. I was off track from all of my original goals starting a family this soon. The back-to-back pregnancies didn't exactly help the intimacy problems, either. We were strained, to be sure.

> *November 12, 1990*
> *I feel exhausted from being pregnant and taking care of Jaede. I hope we're going to be happy in our new condo. We're supposed to move in by December 18. It's going to be a humble Christmas.*

With the close living quarters, the financial strain of purchasing a home, and keeping up appearances for my parents, the pressure had compounded. Kyle and I had our first big argument one night when Jaede woke up crying. I couldn't keep her quiet and this upset him. I ended up spending a good portion of the night in the living room with her where she finally fell asleep.

Kyle and I lacked the communication skills to work through our conflicts. Instead of expressing anger after an argument, he gave me the silent treatment for days. I guess it was his way of avoiding a confrontation, but it left me hurt and confused. I tried to act like everything was normal in front of my parents. I still felt the need to please them, to seek their approval. A part of me still wanted to live up to that perfect ideal that was impressed upon me growing up. Sometimes I even felt the need to fashion my journal entries through these rose-colored glasses.

> *December 10, 1990*
> *We're getting anxious to move into our own place, to have privacy. The pregnancy is going very well. I don't know what the gender of the baby is, but we think it's a boy so far. We are excited, anxious, nervous—lots of mixed emotions!*

During the pregnancy, I began having mysterious dreams about my unborn baby. In these dreams, I saw a small boy with short blond hair and an oblong face. He was still in my womb and seemed frail. When I tried to speak with him, he only looked ahead and said nothing. I couldn't reach him. The dreams occurred a number of times and left me with an unnerving sense of apprehension about this child.

Just after Christmas, we closed escrow, and we were finally able to move into our new condo. We celebrated with a small housewarming party, inviting friends and family to join us in this exciting step in our ladder to success. Big things were happening for us and for the country as well.

> *January 24, 1991*
>
> *Our country went to war eight days ago against Iraq. The economy is a little shaky and Kyle's company is struggling right now. I hope they don't lay him off. Right now we're thinking of starting our own business in case he loses his job. Times are going to be tight, especially with the new baby coming in April. We decided if we have a boy, we're going to name him Quinn.*

The used car we had recently bought started having major problems, smoking profusely every time we drove it and filling the car with fumes. I began to worry the fumes would harm my unborn baby, but we didn't have the money to fix it, and it was our only source of transportation at the time.

> *March 12, 1991*
>
> *I am very anxious for the new baby to come! So far I've gained 32 lbs. That's too much. I want to lose lots of weight after the baby is born so I can look good and start acting again. Maybe I could do some modeling, too. We are still trying to start a business. Kyle wants to take out a business loan and do it all himself, but he isn't quite dedicated enough yet. I think he needs to put more effort into it.*

Kyle attempted to start a small rooftop balloon business as an extra source of income for us. He figured if we had enough balloons rented out each weekend, we could cover the added expense of our new home. Kyle's creative intelligence often inspired me, and his ability to fully develop an original idea in a matter of minutes was impressive. It was one of the things I loved most about him. However, he often struggled with following through on his ideas. Though he started off with what sounded like a great plan, it usually fizzled before it ever saw its completion. Action was the missing link. He referred to himself as a great "idea man." Unfortunately, ideas don't pay the bills, and I was getting nervous about making our new house payment. I clung to my goals and, though they were being modified by my burgeoning family, I still felt that life held so much for us.

> *March 21, 1991*
>
> *I want to start my career. I'm going to be 22 years old in a week and I'm already feeling old. I know I've accomplished a lot since we've been married. In less than 2 ½ years, we will have bought a car, bought a condo, had two children, and started our own business. But there is so much more to do in this lifetime! I'm just feeling anxious. I guess when you're pregnant, the whole world stops until it's over.*

On my next doctor's appointment, I was informed that our insurance had been cancelled.

"Are you sure?" I asked the receptionist, feeling the beginnings of panic. "I know premiums are still being deducted from my husband's paychecks every week. Can you please check again?"

She checked a second time and confirmed that our insurance was cancelled. I left the doctor's office in tears and rushed home.

Kyle and I did some quick research and learned that his employer had been spending our premiums elsewhere since October. The baby was due in two weeks and my doctor was demanding payment in full prior to delivery. When Kyle confronted his employer, he was fired. I was sick with worry and didn't want the baby to feel my stress. I knew labor could happen at any time. We quickly extended the limit on our credit cards to help cover the cost and called the hospital to arrange for a discounted rate for payment in full.

> *May 8, 1991*
> *We had the baby! It was a boy, and he was born April 26 at 7:55 am. We named him Quinn. He's got blue eyes and is so handsome! We are having fun with Quinn, but it's a lot of work, especially with two kids. I can't believe we actually have two kids!*

My labor and delivery with Quinn went smoothly, and there were no complications. He was a healthy baby and almost a pound-and-a-half bigger than Jaede had been. I was excited to have a son and was looking forward to an entirely new experience. My darling Quinn was beautiful and perfectly precious, and my heart embraced him fully.

The nurse who cared for me throughout my labor was the same nurse who had been there with us when Jaede was born. She was amazed we were having another baby so soon and was again impressed with us. We spoke proudly of our little family and our lofty plans. At the end of her shift, she came to say goodbye and told us she would never forget us.

We brought Quinn home the next day and introduced Jaede to her new brother. She didn't really know what to do with him—she herself was still a baby. Now we were unemployed with a new house, a new baby, a fifteen-month old, and thousands of dollars in credit card debt. Kyle didn't know what to do for work, and I had my hands full at home.

June 12, 1991
Quinn is growing so fast. He is definitely bigger than Jaede was at this
age (about six weeks). Jaede is adjusting better to Quinn. Sometimes she
gets jealous, but not as often. They are a lot of work, but we're enjoying
them. Our mortgage went up $200.

Kyle sued his former employer for fraud in small claims court and won.
Collecting the money would take time, something we didn't have much of.
Credit card debt was stacking up faster than we could pay it, our medical bills
were still coming in, and we had just applied for unemployment. Meanwhile,
I co-directed a summer stock theatre production at the local high school
to earn extra money, and Kyle worked to get his rooftop balloon business
launched.

Then another tragedy struck our lives. Kyle's mom was diagnosed with
cancer and was going in for surgery. Her prognosis wasn't good and was
complicated by her other health problems. His parents lived four hundred
miles away, but somehow we needed to find a way to make the trip out there.

* * * * * * *

One night I received a phone call from a former high school friend. She
was working in the entertainment industry as an independent filmmaker,
and we talked for over an hour about her experiences. I was enthralled. I
purposely didn't tell her how things were going for me; it was too depressing.
My children played while I sat back and enjoyed this rare social encounter.

During our conversation, Kyle came home. He had been out with one of
his brothers all day, but when he walked in, he became upset that the house
was a mess. Quinn had spit up all over himself, but I hadn't noticed yet. I
hung up the phone and expressed to Kyle my frustrations with trying to care
for two babies and keep a clean house. I didn't have any kind of a life outside

the home like he did, and it was discouraging. Then he said something I thought I would never hear from him.

"You just haven't accepted your role yet, LeeAnn."

I was speechless.

The force of that statement hit me like a freight train. All the discussions during our relationship about never imposing traditional roles on one another, about helping each other pursue our dreams no matter what, were suddenly struck into a strange, black void. They were meaningless, and I now realized the way he truly felt. This was my role, to be a stay-at-home full-time housewife. This was not what I wanted to do, but I felt trapped. I had two babies and a husband. These were significant responsibilities and I felt the weight of it. I also had a strong sense of obligation and wanted very much to do the right thing. I wasn't sure exactly what that was, but I assumed it must be to support Kyle and be a good wife and mother. I loved him very much and wanted an ideal relationship for us. I was a girl with a dream of happily ever after, and I thought in terms of superlatives. Our marriage would be the greatest marriage ever. So I tucked my heart's yearnings neatly into the far corners of my mind where they would have to stay for now. I buckled down, setting aside all my hopes and interests, and put my full attention to caring for Kyle and our children. I fully assumed my "role." Circumstance was calling me to a more urgent obligation.

Chapter Seven
Distance

It became clear that Kyle's mom was not going to live long. I knew he was distressed over it, and though we didn't have the money to keep making the trips back and forth to see her, we knew we had to. Not knowing where our next check was coming from, I was paranoid to spend money unless it was absolutely necessary.

> *August 15, 1991*
> *Well, finally good news. Kyle made a balloon! He went out and bought the material, equipment, and rented an industrial sewing machine. He has been very busy sewing down in the garage. The balloon is approximately 35 feet tall and fluorescent yellow/green/pink. Kyle still doesn't have a job.*

We now had a small source of income with Kyle's balloon business. He had taken a risk in building something he had never built before and I was so proud of him. Though we had spent nearly all of our money to pay for that first balloon, we were hopeful that it would bring us some relief. Kyle did side work for various family members to supplement his earnings, and an attorney friend of ours agreed to take on our case against Kyle's former employer pro bono. This allowed us the possibility of recouping the medical costs that would have been paid by our insurance. The small claims award had come through, but did not cover all of the expenses.

I enjoyed watching my children grow during this time. At four months old, Quinn was an energetic little boy and was almost as big as Jaede, who was a petite year-and-a-half. She began talking soon after Quinn was born and was fun and engaging, but Quinn preferred being alone with his toys rather than interacting with the rest of us. Parenting was still so new to me, but I had some concerns about Quinn. He couldn't hold anything in his stomach very well. He went through several outfits a day covered with spit up. He also pushed me away whenever I tried to hold him close. I figured that all children were different, though, and he was still so young.

I watched how my two stepsisters handled their own children; parenting seemed almost effortless for them. It was too easy to compare how our babies were developing and I tried not to let the differences bother me. My little sister had no children. She was unmarried and had become somewhat transient. Our communications were few and far between. As different as we were from one another, though, I longed to have someone to talk to; someone who knew me and understood me. But she was inaccessible, both physically and emotionally.

It was my relationship with Kyle that left me wanting at the end of the day.

> *September 13, 1991*
> *I have been feeling a little sad lately. I feel like Kyle doesn't love me as much anymore. He doesn't give me nearly as much attention as he used to. I hug and kiss him a lot, and he doesn't really hug me back. He never initiates affection or sex. It really hurts my feelings because he is the only person I will ever be with. He's always talking about his business ideas. He and his brother talk on the phone for hours at a time. It's like he would rather be with him than with me. I know he is close to his brother and loves him, but I am his wife. I just feel neglected, and I can't tell anyone because they'll think there's something wrong with our marriage. I really don't know what to do. I love Kyle and I just want us to be happy.*

My love for Kyle and my attitude of acceptance prevented me from confronting him about the disappointment I felt in our marriage. It seemed easier to keep my feelings to myself. Besides, I didn't want the silent treatment. I was also sensitive to the stress he was feeling due to his mother's illness. We took another trip to see her and spent as much time as possible there. She loved visiting with Jaede and Quinn, and it was difficult to say goodbye when we left. We planned to go up again the following week, but it was too late. Kyle's mom died two days after we returned home. When the call came, we borrowed money from my parents to make the trip back. The following days were spent in a whirlwind of funeral arrangements, with a grieving family and restless children. It was also the first time I had ever seen Kyle cry.

> *September 26, 1991*
> *I know we need to have faith that things will work out, but it's hard. Every day I feel this huge burden on my back. All these worries are lingering over me.*

Money was scarce, and our lawsuit was dragging on. Our car engine had blown out, and we were now without transportation. Kyle looked for work, but not actively, and my sympathy and devotion to him didn't help. It only served to romanticize the desperate situation we were in. I fed his self-pity and his pride. Through my continued support of his business ideas and my belief in his great potential, I unknowingly encouraged him to avoid menial jobs, and not to take work that was "beneath" him. Because of this, we were unable to pay our bills or support our family.

A few weeks later, however, we received a small inheritance from Kyle's mom's trust, enabling us to get caught up on our bills and to help pay expenses for Kyle's fledgling rooftop balloon business. We also inherited a small share of undeveloped family property out-of-state. Though this money gave us temporary relief, we were still not making ends meet. We celebrated our third anniversary in December and bought only a few small Christmas gifts.

News of our financial situation spread through our church community, and we found ourselves the recipients of several charitable and anonymous donations that holiday season. Anonymous givers left baskets of food and gift bags on our doorstep. It was unexpectedly humbling, and through it, we began to empathize more deeply with the needs of others. We were far from our initial lofty goals set at the beginning of our marriage, but what we were gaining was somehow more significant.

> *December 25, 1991*
> *We have been truly blessed. We really came to realize the importance of giving. Kyle and I realize that we have happiness right now, without having money or great possessions. And when we do finally become successful, we will help others who are in our situation. We already have the most important thing in life right now—our family. I am truly grateful today!*

The New Year arrived and life took on new hope. With money from the second dispersion of the trust, we were able to buy a small used car. Kyle started a part-time job as a construction foreman at a local amusement park, since he hadn't sold a balloon in months. A small window of opportunity for acting presented itself, so I had new headshots taken and began auditioning.

> *January 20, 1992*
> *Jaede is going to be two years old soon! She is growing so fast. She says new words every day. She is absolutely gorgeous! And Quinn is already nine months old. He's not crawling, but I think he'll just go straight to walking.*

Quinn's slow development wasn't too big of a concern yet. *All children progress at different rates,* I reasoned. *He's just a little behind.* There were, however, a few behaviors that concerned me. Quinn didn't babble or coo like other babies did. He growled. It was a raspy, strained growl that made his face turn red and the veins in his neck bulge. I was afraid he would damage his voice, but I couldn't get him to stop. He did this incessantly all day long. His inability to look me in the eye was another concern. His gaze would flutter around the room randomly, purposefully avoiding me. If I held his face, he would squirm away. He also didn't play with toys the way typical babies do. He pressed them against his face and stiffened his muscles until he quivered, or he spun them. He had to test the spin-ability of every toy before playing with it.

That Christmas, we bought him a spice rack and took out the spice jars. All day long he spun it around and around, growling in delight at the monotonous repetition. Getting Quinn to hold still was another challenge; he was a constant buzz of energy. During diaper changes, he straightened his whole body, making it impossible for me to clean him. He had a will like a locomotive, and even at nine months old I struggled to control him.

One night, I sat Quinn on my lap while Kyle readied Jaede for bed. It wasn't often that Quinn let me hold him. This particular night he was unusually calm, and I savored this brief moment with my darling son. His satiny-smooth skin and hearty smile bedazzled me, lighting up his face with a brilliant radiance. His laughter always took my breath away. I turned him around to face me, enabling me to look into his clear blue eyes. He glanced away at first, but I didn't force it. Instead, I acted uninterested just to see what he would do. After a moment, Quinn reached up with his fingertips and began touching the ends of my eyelashes, brushing over them ever so lightly. I held as still as I possibly could, watching his countenance closely for any clue into what he may have been thinking. He became very intent, penetrating his gaze on my lashes and growling steadily for several minutes. But he never once looked into my eyes. He was in a world of his own, hypnotized by an ordinary set of eyelashes.

Shortly after, we had portraits taken of our children at a local studio. When the photos were ready, I rushed over to see them. As soon as they set Quinn's picture in front of me, I froze. His eyes were distant and empty, and there was a blank expression on his face that chilled me. *Who is this child?* I questioned silently. I hadn't noticed it before, but now I saw it clearly: Quinn was nowhere to be found.

When I expressed my concerns to family and friends about it later, they assured me Quinn would grow out of his strange behaviors and catch up in his development. I wanted more than anything to believe he was okay. So I waited and did nothing, hoping he would overcome the strange remoteness that overshadowed him.

Meanwhile, a feeling of fear began to grow in my heart.

PART TWO

Angel Child

CHAPTER EIGHT
Introductions

When I was six years old, my mother took me to a mall to buy new school clothes. After a few hours of shopping, we sat down on a bench to rest. As my mother went through her wallet organizing receipts, I watched people come in and out of the department store. One-by-one, people filed past me, ordinary boys and girls, mothers and fathers. Then a family came out, a mother and her two children, but there was something very different about the teenage daughter. She had big, crooked teeth and a distorted face, and she walked with a severe limp. She made loud, peculiar sounds, and her mother had to assist her.

I sat staring, my eyes glued. I had never before seen anyone like her. I pointed at her and asked my mother what was wrong with her. My mother quickly pulled my arm down and hushed me.

"It isn't nice to stare," she said. "That girl is handicapped."

What's handicapped? I didn't know, but it made her face look weird and her body move in a strange way. I couldn't take my eyes off her. She scared me, and I hoped I would never see anyone like her again.

March 11, 1992
I'm going to be 23 years old in two weeks. I'm not getting any younger, that's for sure. I know I have a lot to be grateful for. I have the greatest family in the world, I am in good health, I have a great home. And I have one more year of life to be grateful for. We are still really struggling financially. I just don't see a solution yet. I do have faith, though. We've made it this far. I love Kyle, sweet Jaede, and little Quinn.

I cared for our children while Kyle worked at the amusement park and did random side jobs. I went on a few local auditions for acting but didn't have the time or opportunity to pursue it more. This weighed heavily on me. I felt that my twenties were the time to get my career in motion, and trying to get something going without Kyle's full support was harder than I thought.

March 16, 1992
I feel sometimes that my personal self is suffering and being neglected. But I'm not exactly sure how to fix that. I just think that right now, I have to re-evaluate my goals and my personal feelings. I feel like I need someone to listen to me and try to help me. I need tender loving care. I need encouragement and support. I need attention. I need love.

I didn't share my concerns with Kyle because I didn't want to burden him. I knew he was overwhelmed with work. He talked about it all the time and I didn't want to add to that. I tried to imagine the weight he was feeling in supporting two children and a wife. The responsibility was much larger than either one of us had bargained for. As the youngest of six children, Kyle had been taken care of by other people his entire life. His new life with me put him on the opposite side of that responsibility. It began to feel as if neither one of us was prepared.

In addition, we were not communicating the way we should have been. I didn't really know how to reach out and ask for help. I had always been too busy caring for the people in my life who needed me. Kyle, too, seemed to gloss over his struggles much of the time. I could see it in his face. Neither of us reached out for the relief we both needed. I found myself more submissive to Kyle since our children were born. This contrasted with my confident and assertive nature prior to our marriage. I had become more passive, resigned to my obligated "role." Kyle and I both had our hands full without complicating things with my personal needs. At least, that's how I felt about it, so I kept the quiet sorrow to myself. Instead, I allowed my journal to be my confidante, my friend, my most intimate companion—everything Kyle should have been.

I celebrated my twenty-third birthday and reaffirmed my desire to be more positive about my situation. Life, though difficult right now, was teaching me some profound lessons.

> *March 28, 1992*
>
> *I know my future holds great things that I will do. In order to accomplish these important things, I need to be prepared. I feel strongly that everything is happening this way for a reason. There is something important about the timing of things right now. I need to find out what it is.*

I knew that my life held great meaning. This was clear to me, despite our situation. *The challenges with Quinn and our finances are just temporary*, I reasoned. It was just a bump along the road to happiness and would soon be over. *The best is yet to come*, I told myself. This would later prove to be true. But I would soon discover that the worst was also yet to come.

I began cleaning my parents' house weekly to earn extra money, and Kyle continued working extra jobs. We also borrowed money from my parents to help make ends meet, but I hated having to do it. Though they offered their help freely, I didn't like them knowing that we were struggling so hard. Most of Kyle's family lived out of state and were not available to help us, so my parents became our only line of defense. It was scary not knowing if we would make our mortgage payment each month. Our pending lawsuit against Kyle's former employer prevented us from qualifying for government assistance, and we were currently getting our food from a local food bank. But we had a roof over our heads, and we had each other. Out of necessity, we put our focus on the things we did have and hoped the rest would take care of itself.

I worked again as co-director of the local summer stock theatre production in the evenings to help pay bills, and took care of Jaede and Quinn during the day while Kyle worked. It was a nice break to get away for a few hours each week. Caring for Quinn was very taxing, and even though Jaede was exceptional for her age, she, too, was still so dependent.

One day while I was showering, Jaede took my wedding ring from off the bathroom counter and began playing with it. When I stepped out of the shower, it was gone. I asked her what she had done with it, but her language was unclear. For days I searched frantically, going through garbage pails, checking under beds and in laundry hampers. I even moved furniture in the hopes that she might have stuffed it under a dresser or behind a nightstand. Kyle helped me search everywhere for it, but it was never found. In its place, I began wearing my mother's wedding band.

I turned inward to find peace as my world was pressing down on me. I sought my mother's spirit for help—for that purifying love that had embraced me so fully. I began thinking more about spirituality, something I had been neglecting for some time. I longed for deeper happiness that wasn't dependent on money or security, a peace that didn't leave me whenever my son broke something or spit up everywhere. I yearned for something solid and enduring. I finally shared this desire with Kyle and, together, we recommitted to our love, shifting our thoughts and our lives to what was truly important. We sought meaning and purpose in our trials, to glean some benefit from our suffering. We had been mostly unemployed for sixteen months now, and we were feeling in tune to the needs of others like never before. Our financial situation had humbled us, diminishing our pride and opening our eyes to a side of life that affects so much of the world, yet one we had previously been immune to: poverty.

We began volunteering in our community in a variety of ways. If we couldn't improve our own circumstances, then we would seek to improve those of others. We didn't have money to give, so we gave of our time and energy. We campaigned for an independent politician, volunteered at a local rescue mission, and helped organize a food drive for a neighboring city. It was so rewarding to relieve the suffering of others, and it opened my eyes in a very vital way.

Then just before Christmas, we had an unexpected delivery for the holidays.

December 21, 1992
Every night for the last 8 days, we have received a gift on our doorstep anonymously. We think someone is doing the 12 Days of Christmas for us. They probably don't know they are literally giving us Christmas this year.

Our "Secret Santas" left gifts for Jaede and Quinn, food, and other goodies. One night we found two hundred dollars tucked in an envelope on the porch. It was a blessing. Our children had presents to open Christmas morning, and we had a tree decorated with ornaments. On Christmas Eve, we left a plate of cookies on the porch for our "Santas" with a note attached. It said we were grateful for their kindness and rare generosity. We never found out who they were.

Once again, a new year was upon us and Kyle and I hoped for better times.

January 17, 1993
We have been having a lot of rain, so it's been impossible for Kyle to do any work. We are easily the worst off we've ever been. We have no money and almost all of our bills are past due. I feel so trapped. We have about $40 in the bank. I just have no idea how we are going to pay our bills. If we can just get through these next couple of months.

We tightened our belts even more as our pantry became more bare. This required me to become more creative in meal planning. Oatmeal was on the menu frequently. Date nights, too, required more creativity. One night, Kyle and I drove up to a local hilltop, sat in our car, and shared a fifty-cent candy bar. We laughed as we overlooked the stunning city lights, slowly savoring the chocolate bar to make it last as long as possible. It was simple and juvenile, but surprisingly enjoyable. We were nowhere near where we hoped to be by now. Life had thrown us for a loop, but still we cherished the togetherness. Just to have an uninterrupted conversation was refreshing. Just to be alone was a gift. We held hands and sat in silence for a long while. Silence, too, was a gift.

* * * * * * *

Kyle began working with his oldest brother in a newly formed window business. They wanted him to head up a new division, though it wouldn't be profitable for several months. Kyle would be required to work for free in the beginning. We felt it was a good opportunity, and Kyle took it. Our mortgage fell a month behind and I continued to feel the squeeze. Jaede turned three, and I braced myself for a surprise development.

> *February 22, 1993*
> *Well, I'm pregnant. This is really bad timing. We have no medical insurance and we have no money. We're in trouble. We're not making ends meet. Up till now I've been able to have faith and feel positive. But it's becoming very difficult to do so anymore. What a life! I'm only 23 years old and I'm already burned out! I just can't handle the stress. I feel like it might adversely affect the baby. I know the kids can sense it.*

Despite our best efforts with birth control, we couldn't seem to prevent pregnancies. During intimacy, I was frequently occupied with concerns about our lack of precaution, making the experience very difficult to enjoy. The constant fear of pregnancy put a serious damper on our already awkward sexual relationship. Kyle didn't seem too worried about it. He was excited to be a dad again and loved having babies around. I realized what a highly fertile combination we were. I didn't know how I would handle another baby. We still couldn't figure Quinn out.

"Hurricane Quinn" swept through the house destroying everything in his path. He was fully mobile now and became a challenge on every front. Like disaster prevention, I put out behavioral "fires" all day long. He struggled with the simplest tasks, like holding a spoon and eating. He still used a bottle because he couldn't hold a cup properly, and he had started to exhibit bizarre eating behaviors like regurgitating his food and playing with it.

Because we were on a tight budget, I used cloth diapers for Quinn. He went through ten or twelve per day. His bowel movements increased when he was particularly excited or over-stimulated, which was frequently. Often the contents of his diaper would spill out onto the carpet and if I didn't get to it soon enough, he would track it all over the house. Our little condo smelled like dirty diapers all the time. It began to be a source of oppression for me. And it was one on a list of many.

March 22, 1993

I'm feeling really discouraged again. I just can't seem to get out from under the pressure. You know, I really love my family, but I am very sad. Every single day is scary, stressful, and discouraging. EVERY DAY. We're going on two years now that we've been basically without a steady income. Here are some of the challenges in my life right now:

1. *We have no dishwasher detergent, so I have to hand wash all our dishes.*
2. *Quinn wears cloth diapers 24 hours a day.*
3. *Our diaper wipes will be gone by tomorrow.*
4. *We have less than $2 in the bank*
5. *There are 5 or 6 companies that want to place a lien on our property for debts.*
6. *My house is a mess!*
7. *Kyle is making no money.*
8. *My life sucks!*

> *I am fed up with this. What we need is relief, relief, relief, relief, relief, relief, relief, relief, relief!*

My twenty-fourth birthday came and went, and things continued to pile up, including the dishes and the laundry. Between caring for Kyle, Jaede, Quinn, and my pregnancy, I could not keep up. The house was always a mess. We still received our food from a food bank, and it had been nearly two years since Kyle had a steady job.

Soon after, a significant turn of events occurred. We settled our lawsuit against Kyle's former employer out of court and received our first settlement check. We paid some personal debts and came current on our bills. The settlement included reimbursement for lost wages due to the breach-of-contract and fraudulent termination, and was scheduled to pay us for two years. It was a miracle. With that possibility, we could get ahead and even buy a house in the next year. Jaede and Quinn needed a yard where they could run and play. Maybe then Quinn would catch up in his development.

In the beginning, I thought I wasn't mothering him the right way. I could hardly put shoes on his feet because his ankle joints were so loose. When I dressed him, his arms just hung limp. He didn't acknowledge when I called his name or respond to my affection. I saw the way other children his age behaved. *Why am I struggling so much with this child? Am I a bad mother?*

Quinn's behaviors alienated me from friends and family. My stepsisters were able to take their children out in public without making a scene. But at the park, I chased Quinn the entire time, pulling rocks out of his mouth and trying to keep him from eating other people's food. At church, he was unruly, and we struggled to contain him every minute so he wouldn't be too disruptive. My parents were compassionate and seemed to sense my frustrations, but most of these concerns I kept to myself. Even our pediatrician assured us there was nothing wrong with Quinn and that he would eventually catch up. Still I felt something was not quite right. *Why is he so different?* It made me feel like I was different. *I've been extremely stressed most of Quinn's life, maybe that's why he's so delayed.* Though I did not share these feelings with anyone, I became convinced I was a bad mother and was the reason for Quinn's deficits.

> *May 20, 1993*
> *We're going to take Quinn to a medical center where they deal with developmental problems in children. We still think Quinn is a genius, and he just needs the right kind of stimulation to come out of his shell. He is a sweetie and we love him.*

We hoped Quinn would one day surprise us and start talking. We heard all kinds of stories from well-meaning family and friends about children who were delayed but who later displayed gifted abilities, or children who spoke their first word at the age of five and became child geniuses. We openly entertained all of these ideas, and Kyle especially was a big proponent. But in my heart, I knew there was something very wrong with my son, and I was eager to get a professional opinion.

I went to my obstetrician regularly for check-ups. My doctor told me I had textbook pregnancies and was in excellent health. I hardly thought about the fact that I was pregnant, though. Besides noticing my expanding belly, I didn't really have time to give attention to the experience. However, I began to sense that my unborn baby was a boy. These impressions were distinct. I also began sensing mysterious impressions about a girl by the name of Faith. This name became very prominent in my mind, gradually growing into a lingering presence, almost an awareness, and I continued to feel it throughout my entire pregnancy.

* * * * * *

In July, we took Quinn to a university medical center for observation. The doctor who examined him was a pediatric neurologist specializing in children with developmental disorders. We brought Quinn into a small room and allowed him to explore his environment, so she could observe his behaviors. The room had a few toys, a chair, and a large table. I kept my eye on the doctor's face as she watched him. I wanted to see her reaction.

Immediately, Quinn began his usual growling, stiffening his body as he became over-stimulated by his new surroundings. He picked up a few toys, but quickly became bored with them. He then climbed onto the table and walked around on his tip-toes. I grabbed him and sat him back down on the floor where he began rocking back and forth against the wall—a behavior he had recently adopted.

I found myself wishing Quinn would act normal for the doctor, so she could give us a thumbs-up on his development. I hoped she would say he was just a typical kid and that there was nothing unusual about his behavior. I wanted her to tell me that my fears and concerns were unfounded. But her face told a different story.

"These behaviors are commonly associated with autism," she began.

She pointed out his obsessive fixation on certain objects, his gaze aversion, and his apparent need for sensory stimulation—the reason for him rocking against the wall.

"I'll run hearing and vision tests before making a final diagnosis," she continued, "but his symptoms are hallmark autism."

I felt a lump in my throat. Even though I knew very little about autism, I knew enough to be scared. She recommended a state-funded organization to do the hearing test, the first step in ruling out other problems.

"I'm giving him a preliminary diagnosis of pervasive developmental disorder," she said. "He'll need to start early intervention—a program for delayed children under the age of three. I'm referring him to a clinical preschool where he can begin speech therapy."

Quinn was over two years old and hadn't yet spoken one word.

We gathered all of the necessary information we needed, paid the doctor, and left. Kyle and I talked the entire way home about the implications of autism for Quinn. Though it was a viable explanation of our son's strange behaviors and delayed development, autism was a scary word neither of us wanted to add to our vocabulary.

Quinn's hearing evaluation tested normal and the next step was starting him in speech therapy. I informed my parents of the preliminary diagnosis and they gave me their love and full support. Now it was a matter of waiting to see what time would reveal.

I had an ultrasound the first week of September, and my doctor determined I was already full term. He also told me I was having a boy. Somehow, I knew that. I was preparing to deliver any day and was finally excited for this new baby. I felt ready. The months had softened my heart toward this pregnancy, and I learned to trust in things I could not see. I subdued the anxiety about Quinn and his potential problems. Those would have to take care of themselves for now. A sense of peace settled on me, like the fall chill that was in the air. As the orange and yellow leaves began to fall, a new season of change began in my life.

September 17, 1993
Yesterday Jaede went over to our neighbor's house. Jaede told her, "My mommy is LeeAnn, my daddy is Kyle, and my brother is an angel." The

neighbor corrected her, "Your brother is Quinn." To which Jaede replied, "Quinn is an angel."

CHAPTER NINE
Signposts on An Eternal Path

Baby Shale was born on September 20. The labor was my longest yet, complicated by the umbilical cord wrapped around the baby's neck. With skillful maneuvering, however, the doctor carefully removed it and completed the delivery. A healthy and beautiful boy with red hair and blue eyes was born to me. As I held him in my arms for the first time, a new surge of excitement filled me. He was so precious and delicate, and I loved him instantly. It was true that these babies held my heartstrings. Motherhood had become a strange and unexpected blessing in my life. Kyle was once again a proud father, cradling his new redheaded son in his arms and beaming with exuberant daddy-pride.

I had a much shorter recovery with this delivery and was up walking around within minutes. My doctor released me early and gave me the option of returning home that day, but I opted to stay the night. I knew this would be my last good night's sleep for a while. The next day, we paid the hospital in full with our credit card. When we informed the nurses of our unemployed status and our self-pay arrangement with the hospital, they snapped into action, filling our bags with complimentary diapers, bottles, formula, and infant supplies.

At home, Jaede was excited to see her new brother. At three-and-a-half, she became a little helper to me, fetching toys for Quinn or a bottle for Shale. She was growing up fast and displayed an uncanny wisdom. The first time she held her new baby brother, Shale, she turned to me and asked, "Where's Faith?"

Quinn barely acknowledged his new brother. He simply wasn't interested, which actually relieved me because he loved the sound of shattering glass on our tile floor entry. *What would he do if he got his hands on baby Shale?* I feared.

Kyle and I had been married less than five years, and life was progressing at an unbelievable speed. We worked to connect Quinn with the services he needed until he had a final diagnosis, but we found that it was impossible to access help for children with special needs unless you knew where to look.

A close friend of ours, who had a daughter with cerebral palsy, mentioned to us one day, "You need to get in touch with the agency that offers resources for families of children with disabilities. And you probably qualify for supplemental income for Quinn."

She had been plugged into the system for several years and gave us the information we needed to start accessing resources such as respite hours, therapies, and further testing.

We contacted the state agency, and they came to our home to perform an assessment on Quinn. A few weeks later, we went to their office to meet with a caseworker and fill out questionnaires about Quinn's behaviors and medical history. Soon after, they called to give me the preliminary assessment results. As I sat on the edge of my bed, the phone clutched tight to my mouth, I noticed my reflection in the dresser mirror across from me: I was nervous.

"Quinn has mental retardation and autism," the caseworker stated.

My grip on the phone tightened; I was white-knuckled and tense. For a moment, I was speechless. *He can't be right,* I thought. *Mental retardation and autism?* I choked out some response and said goodbye. I sat for a long moment, staring at my reflection in the mirror. Then fighting back the tears, I dialed our friend. I told her of my phone conversation and Quinn's preliminary diagnosis. She assured me it was only a formality in order to qualify Quinn for services. This helped me to relax a little and bought me the time I needed to prepare myself for the possibilities I was now facing with my son.

During the weeks that followed, I researched a variety of childhood developmental delays. I read about ways that severe allergies, vaccines, and immunizations, as well as a number of dietary conditions can affect behaviors in children. I searched desperately for anything that was treatable, curable, or otherwise temporary. But the more I observed Quinn, the more I realized this was not temporary. Meanwhile, the demands of home were pulling me in all directions.

> *December 4, 1993*
> *I can't believe it's already Christmas again! This year has gone by so fast. A lot has happened. Quinn has been going to clinical preschool for about two weeks. He is doing slightly better. We love him and hope that he develops normally. We're having a lot of fun with Shale. He is just as cute as ever! He definitely adds a lot of joy to our home. My house is still a mess, but oh well. Life is strange, and unpredictable.*

My body had been in an almost-continuous cycle of pregnancy and lactation in the five years we had been married. All of my original life goals were banished to the back burner indefinitely. I had been redefined. I was a full-time homemaker now, and my home was a chaotic mess. I saw this as a direct reflection of myself, and it was an embarrassment. Reaching out to help others during this time was a way for me to escape my own problems. *If I can relieve suffering on some level for someone else, maybe it will relieve my own suffering.* Though we should have been spending our extra money to pay medical bills, we bought Christmas gifts and donated them to two needy families in our community.

January 1, 1994
Happy New Year! We had a great Christmas. It was fun and rewarding
to help others this year. 1993 was a year of change. We've accomplished a
lot. We are looking forward to a really good 1994.

A quiet uncertainty haunted me as I faced the New Year. Despite my instinctive optimism, a nagging sense of foreboding settled on my heart. Then later that month, I had a dream that changed the way I saw everything.

I dreamed that chaos and calamity erupted everywhere. As I walked the streets, an apocalyptic scene played out before me. Buildings collapsed in a great cloud of suffocating smoke and dust. People scattered frantically, dodging wreckage and falling debris. Across the sky, dark heavy clouds billowed and obscured the ominous red glow of the sun. But I walked calmly along a sidewalk that ran beside a tall stone wall, unfazed by the destruction around me. My husband walked hand-in-hand by my side with his face hidden from my view.

Suddenly I found myself in the back seat of a vehicle traveling at a great speed. My parents sat in the front seat, and my husband sat at my side. I was still unable to see his face. My dad turned to give me a knowing look, as if saying, "Be at peace."

We quickly arrived at a beautiful pavilion surrounded by white light. A marble-like floor and a large water fountain graced the center of this pavilion. Immense joy flowed from everyone as we gathered together in this place of love and light.

Two close friends of mine, adorned in white, approached. They were remarkably peaceful and emanated a quiet wisdom. The wife was especially exquisite, and I perceived that it was due to the challenges she had diligently endured with her husband. Her strength shone like a glow from her countenance and she was the loveliest I had ever seen her. As they passed by me, I was drawn to a mysterious man sitting behind them on the edge of the fountain. He had wavy crimson hair and a stocky build, and he peered deeply into my eyes. I sensed I had known this man before as a kind of beloved primordial friend, and I somehow knew and loved him now. He then gave me a knowing smile, and seemed to say, "Be at peace."

An angelic elderly woman in a long white gown approached next.

"You will now see the woman you knew on earth as Carol," she informed me. My heart immediately leapt with excitement.

She escorted me into a large, expansive room with an immensely tall ceiling. Lights came on successively above us, illuminating our path as we walked into it. The anticipation of seeing my mother again was tremendous. It had been over seven years since my spiritual encounter with her, and I fervently desired to be with her again.

As we walked, I took in the beauty of my surroundings, reflecting on all that I was experiencing—the calm, the clarity, the joy. These luminous individuals all had a message for me. And they were lit with a penetrating wisdom that changed me. In this place of peace, I began to see differently. I marveled at how fast my life had ended. It was so final, so complete. The condo, the cars, the unpaid bills—everything vanished in the blink of an eye. All that mattered now was what I had done with my life. It became clear to me that I had lived well, and that was all that mattered in the end. There was nothing else, absolutely *nothing* else. The finality of it took my breath away. This feeling swept powerfully over me, and I openly wept.

My angelic guide walked ahead of me, and the room grew brighter and brighter. I followed behind, overcome by the emotion of this experience. She then turned and gave me a gentle nod, as if to say, "Be at peace."

I awoke suddenly. Tears soaked my face. I looked around my bedroom, disoriented. My furniture was still there, my condo, my belongings—all of it was still there. And I was still alive. The overwhelming feeling lingered and the realization hit me again: it only mattered how I lived. All my worries about not having a bigger home, a bigger car, or more money seemed petty and frivolous now. These things were temporary and unimportant. How I lived and what I learned was lasting. That was meaningful. And that was all I would take with me in the end.

This new understanding buoyed me up in the following months, giving me a defining sense of purpose. It helped me to see what was truly important and acted as a spiritual net, protecting me from the impending fall I was about to experience with Quinn's final diagnosis.

> *April 9, 1994*
>
> *We think we may have finally discovered what might be wrong with Quinn. Fragile X syndrome is a recent discovery in modern medicine. It is similar to autism. All of the symptoms fit Quinn perfectly. The scariest aspect of this whole discovery is that Fragile X syndrome is a genetic disorder. That means that our other children could have it and Jaede could be a carrier of it. Quinn hasn't been tested yet, but I just know he's got it. There's only time for meaningful experiences and relationships. We need to take joy in all aspects of our lives.*

When I went to dances on the weekends after high school, I frequently ran into a young man with Down Syndrome. He loved to dance and showed up every week all dressed up. He spotted me every time and invariably asked me for a slow dance. Though I felt uncomfortable being so close to him, I danced with him anyway. As he held me in his embrace, he looked me square in the eye with a big, innocent grin. I felt completely transparent in those moments, like he could see right through me. When he spoke, his language was slow and muddled, and the conversation was awkward. But after each dance, he told me he loved me. Not like some cheap pick-up line—he meant it. He really *loved* me. He loved everyone. And he had a genuineness about him that was disarming and truly uncommon.

However, I found myself avoiding him whenever possible.

CHAPTER TEN
Momentum

Quinn went in for a genetic screening at the end of April to confirm the diagnosis of Fragile X syndrome. While we waited for the test results to come back, my desire to help others became even greater. My need for purpose expanded and my spiritual dependence on a power larger than myself deepened. Though I was not aware of the challenges I would yet face, I believe my spirit knew and was preparing for it. Things were happening fast and it was only the beginning.

> *June 15, 1994*
> *On Monday June 6, we found out that Quinn tested positive for Fragile X syndrome. Even though it wasn't a surprise, it was still disappointing. At least now we know what direction to go in. He is our sweet little boy, and we love him.*

The diagnosis of Fragile X syndrome was a ten-ton weight that landed squarely on my shoulders. It was absolute, final, and devastating. Though I knew beforehand that it was a strong possibility, it came crashing down on me nevertheless. It was a strange relief in some ways, too. Now that we knew exactly what was wrong with Quinn, we could work on finding treatments and therapies. I immediately began researching the condition to find out exactly what we were dealing with.

I learned that Fragile X syndrome is a mutation in the DNA of the X chromosome. It appears as extra building material or a "dangling" section on the gene. It can be manifested as a premutation for the carrier of the gene, or a full mutation for someone who is fully affected by the disorder. It is the most common cause of inherited mental impairment and the most common known cause of autism. There were a lot of technical terms I didn't fully understand yet. But I knew that Quinn had the full mutation.

From looking at the course of Fragile X inheritance, it was determined that I was the carrier of the disorder. I had apparently inherited it from my mother, and she from her mother. How many generations this disorder had been passed down through the genes in my family, no one knew. There was no record of it anywhere in my family history, nor did I know the probability of passing it on to my other children.

My little sister was also at risk for being a carrier, and this concerned me. She had struggled emotionally as the years had passed and she became increasingly unstable. She battled substance abuse and distanced herself from our childhood family. An unexpected pregnancy with a disabled child would have been lethal for her. The genetic screening was prohibitively expensive, and the state had only paid for Quinn because he exhibited symptoms. My sister had no medical coverage and no means to pay for the test. The state did not approve any further testing for Jaede or Shale either, and we had no way of knowing whether or not they carried the gene.

We began to question the implications of Fragile X syndrome for our children and future generations. Since the Fragile X mutation was only first discovered a few decades prior, relatively little was known about it. And there was no cure. I wanted to learn all there was to know about it and arm myself with the tools to be a good advocate for my son, but the demands of daily life intruded, and I soon found myself overwhelmed.

A week after Quinn's diagnosis, we listed our condo for sale. We needed to find someplace with more room. We held an open house one Saturday and dropped the children off with a babysitter about five minutes away. No sooner had we returned home when the babysitter called. Quinn had burned his legs with scalding tap water in her bathroom sink. We jumped back in the car and rushed over. When we arrived, she was in tears, frantically running cold water over Quinn's lower body. Blisters had already started to form on his legs, and skin was falling off in long, thin strips. Kyle grabbed him, wrapped him in a towel, and we headed to the urgent care center immediately.

When we pulled into the medical center, Kyle ran in with Quinn in his arms, and I followed close behind.

"My son is burned!" I yelled to the receptionist.

She jumped up and urgently rushed us into a trauma room. Nurses came in and carefully removed the towel, revealing Quinn's legs. I gasped. Large red blisters filled with fluid an inch high covered both legs from his knees to his ankles. Quinn had severe second and third-degree burns. Kyle fought to hold back the tears. A moment later, a doctor came in to examine him.

"What happened here?" he asked suspiciously.

I suddenly felt nervous. He inspected Quinn's injuries, looking over the bubbled skin and raw spots cautiously as we recounted for him what had happened.

"For such severe burns to have been inflicted," he said, "he must have been held down under the hot water."

We were horrified at the accusation. We explained to him about Quinn's disability, but he was determined to find someone to blame. While my son cried in agony awaiting treatment, the doctor took pictures of Quinn's legs and compiled a folder for Child Protective Services. Kyle and I could hardly think straight. We refused to give him the name or number of our babysitter and insisted he treat our son. Quinn was barely conscious. Finally, a compassionate nurse came in and took over, giving Quinn the care he needed.

For two weeks, we went to the medical center daily for bandage changes and special treatments, and for two months afterwards, we did the treatments at home ourselves. It was devastating to watch our little toddler crawling around the house in his wraps. He was barely three years old and had enough challenges already. Though Quinn's scars eventually healed, our emotional scars from the experience remained.

* * * * * * *

In August, we were given the opportunity to house-sit for a friend of ours, and we moved our family into their five-bedroom, 3,500-square-foot house for five weeks. It was so nice to have room for everyone and a yard where our children could play. It also enabled us to keep our condo completely clean while it was listed for sale.

Jaede, now four years old, loved having a room of her own for those five weeks. There were new toys to play with, a huge doll collection, and shelves of children's books. She was a bright, imaginative little girl with a vivid imagination, and her reading skills were just emerging.

Quinn was three and went each day to a special education preschool, a class with other disabled children his age and a two-to-one student-to-staff ratio. He was now in the public education system and received transportation on a handicap-equipped school bus. I was glad for his educational opportunity, but he was so young to be leaving home. When I put him on the bus the first day, I carefully strapped him into his seatbelt and gave him a kiss. He looked around with that innocent, oblivious expression that was becoming his trademark. Then I stepped off the bus and waved from the sidewalk until he was out of sight. Seeing my little boy sitting on that big school bus with other handicapped students broke my heart. For the entire first year he was in school, I stood on the sidewalk and cried every morning as the bus drove away.

At seven months old, Shale was a cute, but unusual, baby. His eyes were crossed, preventing him from focusing properly and eliciting the most curious expressions. He had poor muscle tone in his mouth, which caused him to drool. This also impaired his ability to chew food effectively. Though he wasn't developing as quickly as Jaede had, he also didn't have many of the characteristics Quinn had. Shale smiled a lot and had a cheerful disposition. He was very responsive to affection and would let me cuddle him in my arms for hours. He was happy and engaging nearly all of the time.

Kyle worked full time in his window business and seemed to enjoy the opportunity to utilize his entrepreneurial skills. His income had gradually increased, and he was now able to enjoy a sense of accomplishment.

With Quinn away at school for a few hours, I had a brief respite during the day. It was at this time that I began receiving further impressions about a little girl named Faith. These impressions came to me while making beds in the morning, or doing laundry, or preparing lunch. She was compelling me to take notice of her, drawing me gently toward her in mysterious ways. When I had all of our children together, it distinctly seemed as though someone was missing. I even sensed her spirit hovering silently over me oftentimes, watching me as I went about my daily tasks. Her presence was powerful and unmistakably familiar.

Though I didn't want to admit it, I knew in my heart that I was to be her mother. This possibility scared me. I was in no position to take on another child. Eventually her presence grew more persistent until Kyle began to sense it. He and I discussed the possibility that there was a spirit daughter joined to our family somehow, manifesting herself in that house.

Even Jaede began asking, "When is Faith coming, Mama?"

Every day this angel made herself my constant companion, a phantom child leaving an indelible imprint on my environment. And every day I put the idea of having another baby out of my mind. Finally, when the impressions became too strong to dismiss, I knelt down and pleaded with her that she might please wait. I was still trying to gain my footings with Quinn's disability, I explained, and our finances were barely stabilizing. But I promised her that if she would be patient, I would bring her into the world when I was ready.

After that prayer, the impressions stopped and I felt her presence peacefully withdraw.

* * * * * * *

Once Quinn's burns healed, he began walking again and getting into things he shouldn't. One day he managed to slip out the front door undetected. As soon as I realized he was missing, I darted outside looking for him. A neighbor happened to be walking by just then.

"He better be careful of that dog next door," she warned me. "He bites!"

I panicked and picked up my pace. Though I heard no barking, I approached the house next door cautiously. When I rounded the corner, I witnessed something remarkable, the first of many evidences of Quinn's gifts. He was lying in front of the wrought iron gate that kept the neighbor's dog in, with his hand resting on the bottom rung. He was facing the dog square-on, who sat directly across from Quinn on the opposite side of the gate. The dog's paw rested gently on Quinn's hand. They stared at each other intently, mere inches apart and perfectly still, locked in a silent gaze. I stood watching, mesmerized. *How is he doing that?* A moment later, the dog spotted me, jumped up, and began barking viciously. Quinn got up and skipped back to the house as if nothing had happened.

Maybe he was an angel after all.

When our five weeks of house-sitting were over, we moved back into our condo. We hadn't received one single offer, so we took it off the market. It would have been impossible to keep it presentable for viewing while we were living there again. The economy had taken a downturn, leaving us owing more than it was worth, so we decided to wait it out, hoping real estate values would rebound. Work picked up and was going well, enabling us to pay our bills and gradually reduce our debts. Jaede started preschool and, for the first time in a long time, I had a significant break during the day.

It wasn't often that I pondered my own interests. The circumference of my life encompassed Kyle and our children. All my thoughts and energies went to them, serving them in every way I knew how. I loved Kyle dearly. He was my sweetheart, and I was fully committed to our marriage. Though we had been through difficult times, the excitement of being together still gave me a thrill. Each of our children was precious and beautiful in my eyes, and I felt privileged to be their mother. Having a child with a disability was humbling and it was changing me. Even the mysterious spirit girl held an attachment to my heart somehow; she was a stranger from another sphere who wasn't a stranger at all. These unique individuals formed the core of my existence. Yet I was still there somewhere, a young woman peering into the narrow tunnel that represented her dreams.

One morning, I knelt by my bedside and reached out to my mother's spirit. My spirituality seemed to shift and my eyes were opened. A deeper sense of compassion took hold of me. I began to see a whole new paradigm for my life, possibilities I had never before considered. And a new idea came into my heart.

I want to use my talents to inspire people, to be a source of strength for others. I want to be a woman of purpose in this world, Mom. I understand struggle. I know poverty, and sorrow, and pain. I can use these experiences to give others hope.

Gratitude filled me and a spirit of illumination rested on me.

Show me the way, Mom. Please, show me the way.

CHAPTER ELEVEN
The Dark Undetected

Quinn earned the nickname "Houdini."

We rigged our house with all kinds of latches and gates and locks to keep him out of trouble, but he developed the uncanny ability to manipulate every one of them. He was quarantined to the living room and his bedroom. All other rooms were protected and were off limits because of the potential danger to him. The bathroom, once an outlet for his fascination with water, became unsafe after his burn accident. The kitchen was a scavenger's paradise, and Quinn might gorge himself if left unsupervised in there. The front door was the gateway to the outside world—a place of infinite wonder and unspeakable danger to a disabled little boy. We equipped it with a deadbolt as well as a heavy-duty knob cover. Our master bedroom was also protected by a knob cover, but it was the only room in the house that was not childproofed. I wanted it to be a sanctuary of normalcy for Kyle and me. However, despite the childproof locks on everything, "Houdini" somehow managed to breach them all.

One morning after coming out of the bathroom, I noticed the front door ajar. I quickly ran outside to find Quinn standing on the railing of our second-story balcony, wobbling fifteen feet in the air.

"Quinn!" I screamed and pulled him down, narrowly escaping a fatal disaster. "You can't do that!" But he just looked at me with that oblivious gaze.

Another time, he managed to pull our newest knob cover off the front door and took off running. As soon as I realized it, I flew down the balcony stairs in a panic. Just then, my neighbor came walking up the street with him.

"You'll never believe what just happened!" she said. "Quinn was getting into a car with an older couple! I grabbed him just in time!"

I kept thinking how I had only left Quinn alone for a minute. These were the kinds of things that would happen when I was in the bathroom, or changing Shale's diaper, or getting dressed in the morning. Those brief moments when I took my eyes off Quinn were opportunities for him, and he took advantage of them.

Quinn also began waking during the night in fits of crying and screaming. It took hours to calm him down. Despite his speech therapy and early intervention, he was still non-verbal and couldn't communicate to us what was wrong. He developed a glass-shattering, high-pitched shriek that made my hair stand on end. He employed this deafening shrill whenever he was excited or overly stimulated.

Although he seemed unruly much of the time, there were moments I witnessed transcendent qualities in Quinn. I frequently saw him look up to the corner of the room and smile, as if someone was there. He laughed randomly at times, as if he were seeing some comic apparition. It was evident that Quinn saw things the rest of us didn't. There was something special about this child. His face lit up like a firefly on those rare occasions when he smiled, and his laughter was hearty-to-the-bone. His strange behaviors belied a child so beautiful with his deep, ever-luminous blue eyes. Though distant and mysterious, there was in them something pure and other-worldly.

* * * * * * *

In December, Kyle and I celebrated our sixth anniversary with a trip to Disneyland. It was a blast. We had our picture taken with several Disney characters and jumped from roller coaster to roller coaster all day. We felt like kids again, running around the amusement park in our jeans and sneakers, souvenirs flailing. Getting away from home was an opportunity for us to reconnect and renew our relationship. Unfortunately, alone time was rare for us.

In our small condo, Jaede and Quinn slept in bunk beds in one bedroom, and Shale slept in a crib in our master bedroom, which also doubled as Kyle's home office. And we all shared one bathroom. I tried to toilet train Quinn a number of times, but he didn't have any interest or desire to learn. He produced a dozen or more dirty diapers daily and, together with Shale's diapers, it made for a lot of changes.

Jaede was becoming more independent. She was quite precocious, addressing Kyle and me by our first names. She had curly red hair that framed her petite elf-like face, and her eyes had turned a beautiful green color. She loved leaping around our front room to avoid the "hot lava" and role-playing that she was a superhero with magical powers. Jaede was very spirited and had a unique acceptance for all people. She truly inspired me.

Shale was just over a year old and hadn't spoken one word yet. I adored this little redheaded child, with his alabaster skin and hazel-gray eyes. He would often lie in my arms and fall asleep to the sound of my heartbeat. Shale was a little clumsy and was barely crawling. We attributed these delays to his impaired eyesight and were told by our pediatrician that his vision problems would probably correct themselves within a year. We also felt his development would catch up then.

And then there was Faith, ever present in my thoughts.

January 4, 1995
This is my first journal entry of 1995! A new year—Wow! Kyle and I made our goals for 1995. I feel good about this coming year. I know we will face challenges, but we will also enjoy blessings.

The promise of a new year always excited me. Because of the challenges of daily life, I put a lot of trust in the future. I was constantly looking forward to better times, choosing to look ahead with optimism and hope. And maybe a little bit of denial.

Kyle's work was going extremely well, and we bought a truck, the first new car we had ever owned. We had brought home a record income in December, and finances were abundant. I knew the time was right to fulfill my promise to the little spirit girl waiting to be born. Faith already seemed a part of our family; pregnancy was just a formality at this point. I became pregnant quickly, and the doctor set my due date for October 20. I wasn't sure how I was going to manage caring for the other children while pregnant, but I felt confident I could make it work. My sense of obligation was the driving force in my life, as was my naïve ambition. Both kept me going, and both were dangerous in their own way.

Shale's crossed eyes became increasingly worse during this time. They had not straightened like our pediatrician expected. My heart sank every time I looked at him, and I was very self-conscious about taking him out in public. Our pediatrician told us that the first two years are when a child develops depth perception—the visual ability to see the world in three dimensions—and if his eyes didn't straighten by his second birthday, he would have significantly impaired vision for the rest of his life. His second birthday was fast approaching, and this weighed heavily on me. At eighteen months old, Shale was still not walking.

In our research, we found that corrective surgery on both eyes would cost six thousand dollars. We didn't have that kind of money, but we knew Shale needed the operation. Our lawsuit settlement payments had defaulted and we still had no health insurance. We put in several applications, but the insurance companies didn't like the fact that we had a genetic disability lurking in our genes.

Soon after, the news of Shale's condition hit the grapevine of our local church community, and they rallied the resources to pay for his eye surgery. There was a doctor in our congregation who volunteered to do the procedure at no cost, and the additional expenses would be covered by donations from other anonymous donors. It was a major miracle and we began making arrangements immediately.

March 22, 1995
Things are tight because work has been slow. We haven't been able to pay all of our bills. It's kind of scary. I don't want to go through that experience again.

Work slowed again, and Kyle began coming home every day in a mode of need. Our roller-coaster ride of finances was dipping and it felt like emotional vertigo. I gave him my encouragement to bolster him up, and we talked for hours every day about how to improve his work. Other times he just sat in front of the television randomly flipping through channels, unresponsive to me and the children. He seemed distant at times, in a way detached, and occasionally ambivalent about the struggles the children and I faced on a daily basis. I tried reaching out to him continually, to let him know he had my love and respect. I tried to be who I thought I needed to be for him and for our family. But I knew Kyle felt the strain of our overwhelming situation, and I knew there were times he wanted to escape it all.

One afternoon while driving home from shopping, I noticed Kyle driving a few cars ahead of me returning from work. I sped up to try and get his attention, but as he neared our street, he kept on driving. I turned toward home and arrived a moment later, concerned. It wasn't until a half hour had gone by that he finally came home. *Had he driven around in a daze and just missed the exit?* I wondered. *Had he gone somewhere he didn't want me to know about? Had he been debating whether or not to come home at all?* I never found out, and I never questioned him about it.

Another birthday of mine came and went without much fanfare. At twenty-six years old, my life was a veritable whirlwind. The concerns with Shale's eyes, Quinn's behaviors, Kyle's work, and the pregnancy pressed heavily on me.

June 21, 1995

Shale had his eye surgery about three weeks ago. It was a little scary, but it was a total success! He can see straight now. He is so much more curious, assertive, and coordinated. He's a new child! It seems that a lot of people have wanted to help us recently. I also get the impression that we are highly respected, even admired by others.

Our little family became the object of charity for many people. We found anonymous gifts such as diapers, bags of clothing, and food on our doorstep regularly. We began to hear comments like "I don't know how you do it," and "You guys are so amazing." Our unique situation called attention to itself, and we found ourselves to be an example of success in the face of adversity.

Shale was really enjoying his corrected vision. His curiosity heightened as he began to explore the world around him with newfound confidence. It was strange and wonderful to see him focus straight for the first time ever.

Quinn turned four and seemed to be enjoying school. Because of his high impact in our family, it made me miss him all the more when he was gone. I loved seeing his bright face each day when he came off the bus. He wrapped his small arms around my neck as I carried him into the house each day. It was as close as I ever came to receiving a hug from him. He held a powerful place in my heart.

Jaede, too, was doing well in school. She was five now and was unusually bright. Unfortunately, I was missing so much of her childhood because of my necessary focus on her brothers. I was going to teach her to dream big and praise her for every good thing she did. I was going to take long baths with her and show her in a thousand different ways how much I loved her. That impressionable window of time in Jaede's life was shrinking, robbing us of these important opportunities, and I started to feel I had more than I could handle.

Then I happened to read a book about a family with three disabled children. I couldn't believe such a family existed. I stopped feeling sorry for myself and realized there were other people out there who had it worse than I did. I put my own challenges into perspective and determined I would be more grateful that I had it so easy.

CHAPTER TWELVE

Into the Fire

Shale's second birthday at the end of September was a significant one. His development had not caught up as we had hoped. He learned to walk, but he still had not spoken. And though his coordination improved after his eye surgery, I began noticing unusual behaviors emerging.

Shale played by holding objects close to his face and shaking them. He would open his mouth wide while his face quivered and drool ran down his chin. He became over-stimulated easily and turned bright red like he was having a seizure. Instead of toys, he developed a preference for things such as spoons, pens, or sticks. He put these inedible objects into his mouth, and I had to watch him every minute. His eating habits grew more similar to Quinn's every day. He stuffed his mouth with more food than he could chew, then gagged it up and smeared it around his plate. He was always covered with spit-up food, as was everything he touched. I didn't want to believe there might be something wrong with Shale, too, but I could not make sense of these behaviors. Even though he wasn't exactly like Quinn, he was less and less like Jaede. It was clear that Shale needed to be tested for Fragile X.

October 5, 1995
Today we went to the doctor and found out I'm dilated to 3 centimeters already and the baby's head is very low. My contractions are irregular and infrequent. I don't think I'm in labor yet, but I'm close. We think the baby will come tonight. I feel ready finally.

I went into the hospital that night and, after twenty-two hours of unexpectedly sluggish and emotionally draining labor, my darling Faith was born—a delicate six-pound girl with blue eyes and an unusually quiet cry. The nurses put her immediately on a respirator, due to her blue skin tone and slow reflexes. This was the little girl who had reached out to me. This was the attentive angel I had sensed hovering over me for more than a year now, patiently awaiting her turn. In my arms, I held a very special child who longed for the miraculous adventure of life. Her course was now in motion, and though I didn't know exactly what that would entail, we were so happy to be together at last.

> *October 25, 1995*
>
> *Jaede is so excited to have a baby sister. She loves to hold her. We are all excited to finally have Faith in our family. It has been so busy having four kids. I still can't believe we have four kids! We have not been able to establish any kind of routine yet. It is a miracle that Kyle has been home to help. I could not do this by myself.*

Now that Faith had arrived, we could begin to take care of important things that we had been putting off. We had Shale assessed by the state agency for developmental disorders, and he was tested for Fragile X syndrome. While we awaited the results, we applied for a short sale to sell our condo. The real estate market had declined dramatically, but we needed to get into a bigger place. We also bought a used van to seat all six of us. It was full-sized, bright blue, and entirely too conspicuous for my taste, but it was roomy and would accommodate our special needs.

Kyle turned thirty in December and was transitioning into another career. Meanwhile, our money ran out and our financial situation plummeted. We were unable to pay our mortgage and it went into default. We had paid our maternity doctors' bills with credit cards and were at our limit. Within a few weeks, we fell behind on all our bills. We felt buried. The huge stress of trying to keep the house clean, so that it would show well, only compounded our precarious situation.

Then Shale's test results came back: he had Fragile X syndrome, too. I began to feel trapped and afraid. I now had four children under the age of five, and two of them were disabled. I was only twenty-six years old. Shortly after receiving Shale's diagnosis, our condo went into foreclosure, and I felt the world caving in on me.

> *February 3, 1996*
>
> *These are some of the darkest days of my life. I have never felt so desperate and afraid. Kyle took a side job, but it still won't be enough to pay all our bills. No one has looked at our house in over two weeks. Every day is a struggle. I've been reading a lot lately on Fragile X syndrome and it's not good. I don't know if I can handle the changes that are expected to happen in Quinn and Shale. The prognosis is very disheartening. Any of my own interests have been thrown out the window. I just feel lost. What's going to happen to us?*

Quinn became sick with the flu at the end of February and was home from school for an entire week. He vomited everywhere, but it didn't slow him down; he was still as hyper and disruptive as ever. I was exhausted trying to keep Faith and Shale from getting sick. Fortunately, Jaede was in school during this time.

Quinn was obsessed with taking baths and took several each day. We had turned down our water heater substantially after his burn accident, and we allowed him to lie in the bathtub to watch the water trickle from the faucet. It was a way to keep him entertained and away from Shale and Faith. I was breastfeeding Faith and could hardly sit for two minutes without getting up and pulling Quinn out of some disaster. With him in the tub, I had time to tend to her feedings.

I was also worn out from cleaning the condo continuously. All day long I straightened up after the children, moving through the house like stealth and wiping up spills as they happened. I was like a ninja with a spray bottle. There was still a chance we could avoid foreclosure if we could just sell our home. I was desperate for a buyer and was doing everything I could to make this happen.

One afternoon, Kyle was at work and I was home alone with the children, feeling particularly fatigued. I put Quinn in the bath so I could lie down for a few minutes. I turned on the faucet to a trickle and pulled out the drain plug so there wouldn't be any standing water in the tub. Then I went to go rest on the sofa. After several minutes, I became concerned that I couldn't hear Quinn anymore. I got up to check on him and witnessed a horrible scene: Quinn had painted the entire bathroom in diarrhea. It was everywhere—on the walls, in the tub, all over the floor, the toilet, the faucet, and he was covered from head to toe.

"Quinn! What are you doing?!" I yelled as he swept his dirty fingers over the white tile walls like a paintbrush.

I began crying, frantically grabbing a towel to wipe it up. It was a disgusting mess and the stench was suffocating. I stepped out of the bathroom to retrieve more towels when I witnessed another horrible scene: there was a realtor at our front door. I could see her standing on the porch, waiting to show some poor unsuspecting homebuyer our lovely condo. I pulled myself together as best I could and answered the door.

"Hello there! I'm sorry I didn't call ahead of time," she said politely, "but I'm here with a client and they'd like to see your property."

Visions of brown, dripping walls amid signed escrow papers and a mortgage stamped "Paid in Full" whirled through my head as I smiled back at this neatly dressed woman. *Dare I let her in right now?* A morbid image of her crisp white pantsuit smeared with Quinn's homemade paint crossed my mind momentarily, but I dismissed it. This was no time for practical jokes.

"Certainly," I replied through a painfully fake smile, "just give me a minute."

I closed the door and sprung into action wiping down my son, the Picasso, with a giant wad of paper towels. Once clean, I took him out of the bathroom and set to scrubbing the walls, floor, tub, toilet, and every other surface in that bathroom with lightning speed. I was so frantic my hands were shaking. When I was done, I doused the air with entirely too much air freshener and called the realtor in. I walked them through the house quickly, hoping they wouldn't notice the strange smell in the air.

Moments later, after the disaster had settled and the realtor had gone, Kyle came home. He saw the residual stress on my face and offered to take the children to the park so I could have a break. But it felt ironically too late for that.

Life was getting unbearable, and we needed help. We had kept the details of our distress private from both of our families for fear of alarming them, but now there was nowhere else to turn. My parents were the only ones who lived close enough to step in and help. One evening, after describing for them the impossible anguish of our daily life, from the horror of the bathtub-painting fiasco to the daily vomit and midnight screaming fits, tears fell from their eyes.

"We had no idea," Isabel said.

She and I had warmed to one another as the years had passed. Her chemical imbalance tapered off, and I became more understanding of her condition. Though we had been through so much together, I now turned to her as a mother in my time of need, and she was there for me fully.

My parents sat quietly for several moments searching for the right words to say, something that would give us the hope we so urgently needed. It seemed the situation was bigger than all of us. Then my dad sat back and began to share his thoughts.

"You may be going through a refining process, LeeAnn," he began, "much like silver."

As my dad spoke, I let myself relax for the first time in months. I loved him deeply and had always looked to him for comfort. Even during high school, I could depend on my father to sit up with me and read while I worked into the early morning hours on homework. His eyes would close and he would nod off, but his stalwart presence saved many an important assignment. He had always been there, waiting up after a late-night dance or flickering the porch lights as a gentle warning to me that I was lingering too long over a boyfriend's kiss. I looked to him now with that same childhood trust and longing.

He continued with his intriguing analogy, "The silversmith holds the silver in the middle of the fire where the flame is hottest in order to burn away all the impurities. He stands vigil, watching the entire process very closely and with great care," he said. "If left one moment too long, the silver will be destroyed. However, the silversmith knows the instant the silver is fully refined, for it is then that he can see in it his own image."

My dad paused for a second.

"Only then does he remove it from the furnace," he explained.

Understanding filled my heart.

"The purified silver emerges stronger and refined," he said finally. "It is *perfected*."

This analogy moved me deeply. Though I didn't want to be put through the furnace, I could see that even now, I had changed in many ways. I was humbled, to be sure. My eyes were opened. I had been made starkly aware of struggle and poverty and pain. I saw things by a different light, with a different perspective. Everything in my life was being stripped away and, perhaps by the light of the furnace, things were becoming clearer.

After that night, I began to feel better about life. I stopped stressing about keeping the house clean. I didn't stop cleaning it, I just didn't stress about it anymore. My parents had become a glimmer in my darkness—a source of true hope. They had not known how to give me the nurturing or acceptance I so badly needed growing up after my mother's death. In fact, they had pushed me away while trying so staunchly to hold me tight. But now, in this new relationship as an adult, I found the love and understanding I had needed all along. I found the strength and support to see me through the fire.

Also during this time, Isabel took great interest in my sons and their disability, doing her own research into Fragile X syndrome and autism. Her efforts were a substantial help to me and our relationship blossomed. I began to see in her not just a stepmom, but a woman with feelings and interests and talents. She had needs and hopes and dreams, like I had. She had struggles of her own. We weren't so different after all. I realized how much I loved her and she became one of my dearest friends.

We were somehow able to pay our bills with the money from Kyle's various side jobs. Quinn returned to school and life mellowed a bit. Though we didn't receive any offers on our condo, I stopped worrying about it. We obtained our food from a food bank again, and our church helped pay for Quinn's special needs childcare.

March 10, 1996
Faith is so sweet. We are just in love with her. She has brought so much fun and happiness into our home.

I adored Faith and her dainty little presence. She was so delicate and beautiful, a perfect receptacle for my love. I felt saddened bringing her into the rowdy environment that was our home. There were times when she seemed like a glass sculpture in a batting cage. But she, too, adapted.

I turned twenty-seven at the end of March. The children were growing fast and it felt like we were bursting at the seams. Kyle and I made it through the dark days with a sense of humor developed out of necessity.

It was our underlying defense mechanism, our method of self-preservation, subconsciously cultivated as a means of protection against the hopelessness. Things had become so bad it was ridiculous, and that's what made it so funny. With Shale and Quinn cruising around the house in nothing but diapers—like natives in loincloths, Faith sitting in her baby seat watching the spectacle with wide eyes, and Jaede talking away as loud as she could to compete with all the commotion, there was only one thing to do: *laugh*. We made up all kinds of nicknames and catchphrases for our children. To keep from going crazy, we had to mock the horrific things our sons did and the grotesque messes they made. Toilet humor became a staple in our home, as did songs with spoofed lyrics about Quinn's animalistic eating habits and Shale's marathon diaper changes.

Our poverty hit a new level, and our humble cuisine went from oatmeal to ramen noodles for days at a time. I became so inventive at creating something edible from an increasingly dwindling food supply, I began to consider it a hidden talent. Fifty-cent-candy-bar-dates became the standard for Kyle and me, but only when a charitable family member offered to take on the deadly task of free babysitting. And we had all graduated from thrift-store clothing to donated hand-me-downs. We were like the urban hillbillies of Yuppieville.

In April, Kyle and I attended a Fragile X conference in Los Angeles. We brought Faith with us while my stepmom babysat our other children. We gathered information and attended several workshops. It was very eye opening. Many of the doctors I had met with since Quinn's diagnosis had never even heard of Fragile X syndrome. Even though it was estimated that many children with autism also have Fragile X, these children were not being tested for it because it was not widely known. I wondered how many autistic children out there had Fragile X syndrome. I was frustrated by the lack of information being given to the medical community in general, but I was impressed by the doctors at the conference who were being informed about this little-known yet common genetic disorder.

We also met with other parents of children with Fragile X and learned of their experiences. Many of these children had developed verbal language. Quinn was now five, and I wondered if he would ever talk. Shale was two-and-a-half and hadn't yet spoken one word.

I was quickly becoming part of this other community—a community of people from all walks of life. We spoke in different terms, used a different lingo, and existed in a different place than the rest of the world. It was a place of sorrow and loss, a place of unique and unusual experiences. It was a place of miracles, where success was not measured by established milestones or social achievements, but by seemingly small and almost imperceptible accomplishments. It was a community of individuals united by a common experience, driven by a common cause, and changed by a most uncommon gift. I felt I had finally found someplace where I was accepted and understood. Here, I was one of them. And I was not alone anymore.

> *April 28, 1996*
> *We only have three more weeks until our house is auctioned. We will have to find another place to live before then. We don't have enough money to pay rent right now. To be truthful, I am a little scared.*

The fire was getting hotter as we urgently looked for a place to live. At the last minute, we received the first and only offer on our condo. It came in at thirty thousand dollars less than what we owed. We held our breath, hoping the bank would accept it, to prevent a foreclosure and protect our credit rating. But the bank rejected the offer, and we were down to one week before we had to be out.

In addition to juggling our troubled finances and potential homelessness, I was still busy caring for our four children in our tiny condo. Every day was a challenge. I felt the responsibility of raising children like a half-ton weight on my shoulders. I also felt the failure of my efforts. No matter how hard I worked to care for them, my children were being raised in an environment of stress, disorder, and chaos. It was not physically possible for me to meet everyone's needs.

Quinn required the most effort and therefore warranted the most attention. He was a yelling, throwing, escaping five-year-old tornado who produced a half-dozen bowel movements a day into diapers made for a two-year-old. He ate constantly, consuming a steady flow of food from our shrinking supply, only to gag it up and then stuff it in his mouth again.

Shale demanded the next portion of my attention. With his extra sensitive gag reflex he, too, would throw up on a daily basis—particularly during mealtime. This made for a very unappetizing eating experience for all of us. Shale also produced an unusually high number of bowel movements each day. In addition, he needed to be constantly protected from Quinn's aggressive outbursts, which invariably reduced this two-and-a-half-year-old to tears.

Next in line was Faith, my frail seven-month-old baby girl. I imagined she didn't know what to make of the home she found herself in. She was very timid and insisted I hold her all the time. She, too, was not developing as she should and this concerned me. Her only verbal attempts were random animal sounds and imitations of her brother's strange outbursts. And, of course, she contributed to the mountain of diapers I had to change twenty-four hours a day.

Jaede, at six years old, was the last of our children to get my attention. Because she took care of herself so well and required so little supervision, that's exactly what she was given. Her spirited personality and love of life were an inspiration to me, though, and I mourned the fact that I couldn't enjoy my enchanting little redheaded daughter more.

And then there was Kyle. It seemed at times as though there were no two individuals as close as we were. Other times, it felt like we were eons apart. The more intense our situation grew, the deeper he seemed to withdraw from us. He struggled to support our family or provide emotional support of any kind for me. He didn't seem able to see my suffering, or to offer me the kind of love I needed as his wife. I knew he had his own difficult journey to forge, but he depleted my inner resources as much or more than the children did. He talked constantly about work—his frustrations, his ideas, and how unfair it was that he wasn't more successful. I listened and listened and listened until I couldn't think straight. I wanted to wake him up to what was happening right in front of him, to our family, and the pain the rest of us were feeling. But he often seemed removed from it somehow. Still, I loved him deeply, devotedly, even blindly. All the hope and determination I had once put into my career aspirations, I now put into my marriage and family. It would be a success no matter the cost. And the cost was becoming alarmingly high. I was a giver and Kyle was a taker, and our relationship was terribly off balance. We were both after something elusive, yet continually haunted by our persistent pursuit of it.

Finally, there was me. I was no one's priority, not even my own.

CHAPTER THIRTEEN
Hope Is Now

May 21, 1996
On Saturday night, I was laying awake in bed thinking about our situation. I realized that for the past six months we have been hoping for the best, but we had not prepared for the worst. I think the worst would be for us to move into an apartment for a few months. It seems incredible that things could go from bad to worse. We are having Faith tested for Fragile X syndrome. We have some concerns. I hope she doesn't have it.

Faith's development was definitely delayed. She was not like Jaede had been as a baby. This was the only comparison I could make to a typical developing child. Faith often sat on my lap with her hands clasped tightly together, wearing an unusually tense expression on her face. She was anxious most of the time, rarely engaging or playful. I thought maybe it was her environment that was contributing to her behavior. I had read that Fragile X syndrome does not affect girls as often or as severely as it does boys. *Besides, what are the odds that she would be disabled, too?* I rationalized. *God wouldn't do that to us.* Because Faith displayed obvious delays, however, we had her evaluated at nine months old by the state agency that assessed Quinn and Shale.

May 26, 1996
Our plan right now is to move into an apartment on Saturday, June 1. That's where we lived 7 years ago. We're right back where we started. I can't believe we're going to live some place smaller! Everybody we talk to

can't believe we do what we do. I don't even know how we do it. These certainly are strange days.

P.S. We just got a handicap parking placard.

We had come full circle. We were now living in the same apartment building we had lived in as newlyweds seven years before. The apartment had two small bedrooms, two bathrooms, and a microscopic patio, all under nine hundred square feet. Jaede was crammed into a small bedroom with Quinn and Shale who slept in bunk beds a few feet away, and Kyle and I shared a tiny master bedroom with baby Faith. It was humbling to be back at such modest beginnings, a million miles away from our original goals.

In the summer, Kyle hired on with a new company doing residential and commercial replacement windows. It was becoming his area of expertise. He took business trips to various states and was gone for days at a time. These trips were an opportunity to boost his contacts and establish himself as a player in the industry. Even though it was a tremendous sacrifice for me to go it alone with the children while he was gone, we both felt it was worth the potential benefits to our family. I wanted Kyle to have the success he always talked about.

August 18, 1996
Summer school is out, so I'll be home with all four kids for the next 2-1/2 weeks. It's going to be grueling. It gets frustrating living in this apartment, especially when so many of our things are packed away in storage. It just seems that we have an unusually big burden on us right now.

One day, a friend of mine sat down next to me at church and exclaimed, "I don't know how you do it!"

Without even thinking, I replied, "Survival instinct."

She burst out laughing, but I wasn't joking. I had come to a state of survival without realizing it. It was a way of life and I was adapting to it. This is not to say it was easy. My weight dropped rapidly while living in that apartment. Loved ones approached me with concern over my weight loss. They warned me I might have a nervous breakdown if I kept up like this. They recommended I consider taking medication to help me deal with the stress. But I was adamantly opposed to medication and assured them I was fine.

I wasn't fine.

One morning I awoke nauseated and light-headed, barely able to lift my head off the pillow. Kyle was gone for the day, and I could hear the children in the next room waiting to be fed. I fumbled for my robe and staggered out of the bedroom. I put together a quick breakfast for them, then made myself a cup of herbal tea. Suddenly the room started to spin, and I almost passed out. I knew I was in trouble.

I quickly called a woman who had been assigned by our church to visit with me regularly. Amazingly, she dropped everything and came right over. When she arrived, I handed her my tea, went into my bedroom, and crashed for the remainder of the day. She stayed until the afternoon when my stepmom was able to come. When Isabel finally arrived, the woman remarked, "Now I know why LeeAnn is so skinny. I've been stirring the same cup of tea for three hours and haven't taken one sip!"

That day, for a brief time, someone else had an inkling of what I did every day.

I was deeply moved by the charity of countless people who came into my life during those dark days. The compassionate service being rendered on my behalf truly opened my eyes to the needs of us all. I couldn't manage alone, and it wasn't for the lack of trying. I always insisted on getting through difficult situations on my own. I was strong, or felt I had to be. But now I was leaning on others like never before. And though it was difficult to do so, it was a blessing. I needed that help more than I realized.

September 4, 1996

I just got the call from the geneticist who tested Faith. He said she is affected; she has the full mutation of Fragile X syndrome. I can't believe it. It seems unreal, like it's too much for one family. Getting Faith's results has been the most difficult by far. She was the last hope. And now I can't begin to figure out how we are going to manage these children. What does the future hold for us? I just hope we can endure it. It's lonely being the mother of disabled children.

Faith's diagnosis hit me hard. To have thought that I knew what God would or would not do seemed painfully presumptuous of me now. My assumption that He wouldn't give us three disabled children was like daring Him to sink the Titanic. And there was nothing I could do to stop it. So I threw down my anchor, strapped in, and held on. I was going deeper into survival mode, but inside I was sinking.

Friends, family, and the community banded together to get us the help we needed. We qualified for respite hours and free diapers, clothing, sundries, high chairs, and volunteers for childcare, and still it was not enough. It felt weird to be the object of so much charity. Although we were held in very high esteem by these people, it was extremely difficult not being in control of our own lives. We were in the middle of something larger than ourselves, and we braced for impact.

November 8, 1996

We are strapped financially, not able to afford even the necessities of life. We are at a point where we are just surviving. Quinn wakes up regularly each night, sometimes staying awake after only 3 a.m. or 4 a.m. Faith also wakes up every night. I don't hesitate to say that now is the most difficult and challenging time of my life thus far. Everything we ever dreamed of or hoped for has been shattered.

Every morning I woke up with a knot in my stomach. I faced each day with fear. It was all I could do to just go through the motions.

> *November 16, 1996*
> *Why would God send us these disabled children without providing a way for us to care for them? We've done all we can do and it isn't enough. I'm getting older way too fast. I can feel myself aging—physically and emotionally—and it scares me. What have we done to deserve this? Are we being punished? The fact is that I can't take this kind of existence anymore.*

> *December 14, 1996*
> *We're in the heat of the fire right now. Things are intense. I think I might be getting an ulcer. These next few weeks and maybe months are going to be seeing what we're made of. I hope I can last long enough.*
> *P.S. One year ago we thought we had reached our limit. We thought we couldn't handle any more. Well, it's been a whole year.*

> *January 2, 1997*
> *The kids have been sick for about two weeks, and now Kyle is sick. I feel like I'm doing the work of ten people right now. We need help. We need a miracle. This oppression is having lasting effects on me. I'm losing something deep within. And it feels like the walls are closing in on us. All I know is I hate my life. This is not a life. This is hell.*

My home was a madhouse. The noise level was staggering. There was a constant flow of Quinn's growls, Shale's monotonous moans, and Faith's imitations of her brothers. And they were all competing with each other. The television played a continuous series of animated musicals to keep the children entertained. There was food everywhere. Their Fragile X metabolisms were lightning swift and I couldn't feed them fast enough. Because of Quinn's sensitivities with certain textures, he ate only dry foods such as toast, cereal, or crackers. I felt like I was drowning in a sea of crumbs. I vacuumed two or three times a day to clean up the mess. We had to replace our vacuum cleaner every year.

Our team of advocates included schoolteachers, respite providers, local church leaders, state agency caseworkers, and my parents—who all worked hard to get us extra help. They also researched what assistance was available to families like ours. While living in the condo, we had applied for supplemental security income for our disabled children but we were still awaiting approval. Our caseworker put us at the top of her one-hundred-and-fifty-family caseload and became one of our biggest advocates.

I was caught up in the vortex of the special needs universe. There were meetings, phone calls, visits, and paperwork, in addition to the demands of the children. There wasn't time to blink. But every night at bedtime, I made the time to sing to Jaede and scratch her back softly. This is something she loved me to do for her. No matter how spent I was at the end of the day, I made sure I did this for Jaede.

One night when I went in, she was particularly distraught. Quinn and Shale were asleep on their bunk beds just inches away. We spoke softly so as not to wake them.

"Mom, I can't even bring my friends over because Quinn and Shale are so embarrassing," she whispered emphatically. "I don't like having handicapped brothers."

I couldn't blame her. Jaede was all too aware of our unique situation. She was practically the third parent in the house, a big responsibility for a seven-year-old. I crawled under the covers and cuddled up close to her. *Maybe tonight I'll linger a little longer*, I thought.

"Why can't we do what normal families do?" she continued. "Why don't we go to the movies, or the park, or play at the pool like my friends? Why do my brothers have to ruin everything? They're always messing up my stuff and taking my things. It isn't fair, Mom. You do everything for them. I don't get anything."

She cried and I held her in my arms.

"Jaede," I began gently, "I want you to know that it isn't easy for your brothers either. They have challenges, too."

She nuzzled in closer to me, and I pressed her to my heart.

"Quinn and Shale will never have friends like you have," I continued. "They will never go bike riding or play sports. They will never read a book or sing a song. They can't even talk. You're a very lucky girl to be able to do these things. When they turn sixteen, they won't be getting their driver's license or hanging out with friends like you will. They won't ever date or go to a prom. And they'll never fall in love . . . "

My voice trailed off and a strange sadness pierced my heart. I suddenly realized the impact of my sons' disabilities in all its implications. I would never see them receive a school award or sing in a school play. I would never see them dance or tell a story or wave good-bye. I wouldn't see them graduate from high school, or live independently, or get married. And I would never hear them utter the words, "I love you, Mom." These experiences would never be mine. *Never*. And for the first time, I truly felt the loss.

Outside our window, there were other homes where little boys were telling their parents goodnight, maybe giving them kisses and hugs, perhaps talking of the events of their day, and going to sleep in the knowledge that they would be waking up to do all the normal things little boys do. But inside our home, there were two struggling boys trapped inside defective bodies and impaired minds who would never know such experiences. As we lay there in that cramped, quiet bedroom, my little girl held me in her arms. And we both wept.

My heart changed forever that night. The experience with Jaede left me with a profound sense of gratitude for all the things we usually take for granted, like being able to talk, to read, to learn, and to love. I vowed

I would never forget these things or how I felt that night. I determined to never dismiss or belittle the blessings in my life, however seemingly small. I promised myself that I would be grateful for all the things my children *could* do, for their simple and hard-earned milestones. Maybe they couldn't talk, but they could smile, and laugh, and be loved.

And that was worth more than any words they could ever say.

My mother, Carol, in her high school band uniform. I found this vivacious picture of her in the set of heirloom scrapbooks I inherited from my dad. She is holding the same clarinet on which she later used to play Moonlight Sonata, her favorite song.

My mother's senior picture, class of 1963. She was seventeen years old and had her whole life ahead of her.

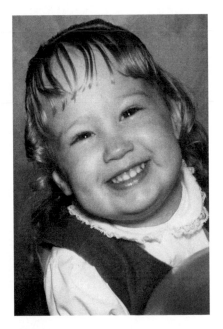

The faculty picture from my mother's scrapbook where I discovered her empty eyes and labored smile. She is only twenty-nine years old here. She had aged dramatically and would soon be diagnosed with cancer.

A little girl with stars in her eyes: here I am at age two.

With my dad, Lemoyne, and stepmom, Isabel, at my high school graduation, 1987. I am wearing the prestigious performing arts medallion around my neck.

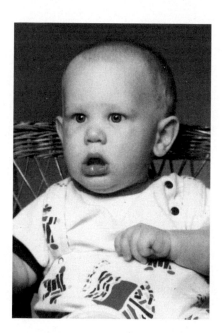

The baby portrait of my son, Quinn, that chilled me the first time I saw it. His eyes were blank, an indication that would later become a distinguishing feature of his expressions.

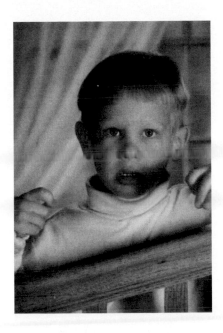

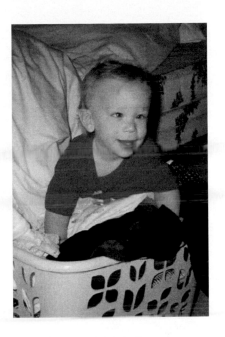

Quinn in his first grade school picture. He often seemed as if in his own world.

Shale plays in a basket of laundry, about eighteen months old here. His eyes were crossed for the first two years of his life, resulting in permanently impaired vision. I had not yet detected his disability at the time this picture was taken.

Always the protective older sister, Jaede at three years old, and Quinn at two, sit together on mommy's rocking chair in our little condo. From the beginning, Jaede shared a rare closeness with Quinn that remains to this day.

From left, Jaede poses for the camera while her disabled younger siblings Quinn, Shale, and Faith wait to be fed.

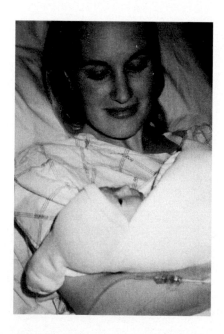

The little angel who persisted in making her presence known to me, Faith's birth was a happy reunion. She would be diagnosed with Fragile X syndrome nine months later.

After receiving Faith's diagnosis, my weight dropped dramatically due to profound stress. I weighed barely 100 pounds in this photograph.

Here with my "miracle baby," Psalm, tucked in my sweater, about six months old in this picture. I had recently learned she did not carry the Fragile X gene. Her unplanned birth would be an accident-turned-blessing in our lives.

Shale in mid-air, bouncing on the trampoline. He indulged in this sensory stimulation frequently—a delightful treat for this seven year old.

Joining Quinn in the wagon, I'm singing "Three Little Monkeys Jumping on the Bed," his favorite song. Faith joins in the fun, too.

A typical day of chaos in our house. I strap the video cabinet shut, while Faith, Shale, and Psalm play on strewn sofa cushions. I was living in survival mode.

Shale and Quinn play on the sofa in our Utah house. Wearing one-piece jumpsuits was the only way to keep them from completely undressing throughout the day. Behind them is part of the gate system we built to limit their access to the kitchen.

Christmas morning 2002. Twelve year old Jaede gives me an affirming hug while Faith plays coy for the camera. Just two weeks prior, I had nearly crashed my van full of children into an icy underpass to end our suffering.

A turning point: Dan and I at our beautiful wedding, June 7, 2003. I was starting a hope-filled new life.

Shale, 14, and Quinn, 16. Though they are usually incompatible, here they make rare contact for a brief moment.

Our family today, from left: Psalm 13, Dan's daughter Erika 18, Shale 19, me, Dan, Quinn 21, Jaede 22, and Faith 17. (Dan's son, Alex 22, is not pictured) The miracles continue.

PART THREE

Out of the Darkness Came the Light

CHAPTER FOURTEEN
Turning to the Sun

January 12, 1997
Today I have actually felt good. In fact, for the last several days Kyle and I have both felt good. We experienced a change of heart. Nothing in our circumstance changed, but we feel lighter and happier. Now we are at least facing the future with courage and hope. We had been blinded by despair. Now we can see again.

In February, our caseworker called to tell us about a possible opening in an excellent group home for children with disabilities. Kyle and I were initially opposed to the idea of placing Quinn in a professional home. But as we thought about it over the following days, we began to feel that this could be an opportunity to teach Quinn some of the skills we couldn't teach him at home, such as toilet training and behavior management. If he could go in for just one year, we would have enough time to stabilize our situation, so he could return home to a more structured environment. If he were to qualify for a level-four group home—reserved for the most challenging children—he would then be eligible for full-time respite hours when he returned home. This was another incentive for placing Quinn.

Kyle, Quinn, and I made the thirty-mile drive to see the group home. We had never been to one before and weren't sure what to expect. As soon as I walked in, I knew Quinn would be happy there. In fact, Quinn ran right into the entertainment room and began playing. It was a beautiful two-story facility with five bedrooms and a huge backyard complete with a trampoline and swing set. The entire house was designed to accommodate special needs: alarms on all the bedroom doors, an intercom system throughout, latches on all the cabinets, special needs toilet attachments, an electronic gate in the front yard, and a high wall in the backyard. They even had a fully trained staff, and a housekeeper who made the beds and emptied the diaper pails every morning. I was surprisingly impressed.

We returned home excited—something we hadn't felt in a long time. We sat down to begin to arrange placement for Quinn as soon as possible. While he was away, we would make preparations for an organized and structured home environment for him to return home to. We had a lot to do, and only a few months in which to do it.

My parents were a tremendous help during this time, offering support, giving their love, and even making phone calls and researching organizations that could help us get into a house designed for special needs. The community and church support dwindled. People went back to their normal, comfortable lives, but Kyle and I pressed on.

Our caseworker worked vigilantly to reserve Quinn a spot in the group home. The process was a lengthy one. State and federal funds, thousands of dollars worth per month, would pay for it. It amazed me how much money the government was willing to throw at a handicapped child living outside the home, but there was precious little available for that child living *in* the home. There were all kinds of resources and services for the child who was placed, but my three disabled children at home received minimal help from these same organizations. It seemed ironic.

April 6, 1997
I have changed so much in the last eight years that I feel I could write a book about it all. In looking over the span of the last six years, which this journal encompasses, I can see the wisdom of God in letting me pass through adversity and pain. I don't know what the future holds, or even

what will happen tomorrow. But I do know that what I have overcome and what I am now enduring is preparing me for an interesting, if not exciting, future. I'll be ready.

I closed out the journal that held the last six years of our marriage, the four children born to us, and our roller-coaster life so far. I hoped it marked the close of an era, the end of the suffering we had endured, and the horrific moments we had survived. Somehow, it seemed to symbolize the deep and unexpected transformation that still gripped me.

It represented the fire.

Then, a few days later, a miracle happened. Somehow, through divine means I did not fully understand, my burdens lifted. That invisible weight I had carried for years was removed from my shoulders. This experience was infinitely more massive than the change of heart I had recently felt. Like strong arms reaching down from heaven and scooping me up in their gentle embrace, my sorrows swept away completely, and I was released from the darkness that held me captive. I felt a degree of relief so exquisite, I wept with gratitude. I also felt a confirmation in my heart that I had been given all the tools necessary to endure my challenges. A strong impression filled me that everything was going to be okay, no matter the outcome, and that I could be happy simply *because.* It was a message of hope from beyond, a light shining in the darkness, infusing my spirit with its rays. I finally relinquished my fears, my worries, and my sadness. I felt them all vanish, leaving me weightless.

Immediately, doors began opening for us, and Quinn was accepted into the group home.

June 16, 1997
We are preparing to take Quinn to the group home in July. We know it's a great opportunity for him, but we have mixed emotions about it. We

need the break and it will be a relief. But we will miss him terribly. Life will definitely be different—for all of us.

One after another, remarkable things began happening. We sold the property we had inherited from Kyle's mother's trust and were able to pay off our debts. Kyle was offered two new job opportunities, and we began to see a way out of our dire situation. Our caseworker arranged for us to receive two new handicap-equipped strollers and two new special needs car seats for Quinn and Shale, and we had a harness strap installed in our van that would keep Quinn safely in his seat—all donated gifts. The blessings flowed and we just sat back and marveled.

Quinn's placement date was fast approaching, and a myriad of emotions confronted me. Though he was six years old, developmentally Quinn was still a baby. He was nonverbal and completely dependent. If something bad were to happen to him at the group home, he would have no way of telling us. In two weeks, we would send our little boy to live with strangers, entrusting them with our most cherished treasure. And in the coming nights, my son would be tucked in by a different mother. It was a lot to think about.

Since children with Fragile X syndrome often suffer from seizures, and Quinn had displayed some of the related symptoms, he was scheduled for an EEG prior to entering the group home. We arranged a babysitter for our other three children, so Kyle and I could both accompany him to the testing.

When we arrived at the hospital, Quinn became angry. We quickly checked into the room where he would be tested, and the nurse wrapped his body in a special medical papoose to keep him still. He immediately grew panicky and began crying. She then carefully placed a cap on his head and hooked up the electrodes to the monitor. But Quinn's sensory stimulation was overloaded, and he would not hold still. I feared it would be impossible for the nurse to get an accurate reading. She stepped out of the room momentarily, and Kyle and I said a quick prayer for Quinn, pleading that he would cooperate so the nurse could complete the test effectively. Instantly Quinn calmed down, and by the time the nurse returned, he was fast asleep. She remarked how unusual it was for someone to enter REM sleep so fast. I knew I had witnessed a miracle. Quinn truly was an angel.

The test was successful and it was determined that he did not have seizures. We returned home and enjoyed our final hours with Quinn as a family.

> *July 14, 1997*
>
> *This is a day to remember—one of the most important days of my life. We took Quinn to the group home tonight and dropped him off. We know it is a great opportunity for him, but it is difficult for us. We will miss him deeply. We love him so much. I feel strongly now that I don't want him gone long.*

As we stood with Quinn in the doorway of the group home, I felt a sharp pang that only a mother can know. I was not prepared for the separation just yet. Maybe I never would be. The staff took his luggage quickly as if to hurry us through this heart-wrenching goodbye.

"It will make it easier," they told us.

There is nothing easy about this, I wanted to say.

Inside, children laughed and played. My son was excited to join them and was anxious to go in. I quickly reminded myself of all the reasons why we were placing Quinn in professional care: we had to do it for our own sanity. The stress had become unbearable. Jaede would have more of a normal home and could be a kid again. Shale would have the peace he so desperately needed. Faith could begin talking and catch up in her development. Finally, Kyle and I could replenish our relationship. There would be more sleep, more peace, and more time. Still I hesitated.

The staff gently urged us to say goodbye while Quinn pulled on our hands, eager to go in. Jaede, Shale, and Faith stood by, restless. We leaned over and gave our little six-year-old boy a few unreciprocated hugs and kisses, and then we released him into the arms of his new caregivers. He didn't even look back.

As we turned down the walkway toward the electronic gate, the sun slipped behind the horizon, pushing the warm summer evening into night. The calm warmth in the air seemed to mock the cold conflict I felt in leaving my sweet angel behind. *Will Quinn miss us? Will he long to be with his family again? Will he think of me while we're apart?* But inside I already knew the answers. And though it hurt, I knew it was a blessing.

CHAPTER FIFTEEN
Miracle

August 6, 1997
Quinn has been gone about three weeks. We miss him, but he is doing
well. Life has been a lot different around here, a lot quieter and calmer.
I've started writing poetry again.

The emotions of my new experience began to reconnect with the deepest
part of me, juxtaposing hope and a bitter longing in my emerging creative
mind. Poetry was a powerful way for me to articulate how I felt about it all.
I took my unique experiences, put them into words, and with them, created
a lasting snapshot of my soul.

Miracles continued to flow into our lives. In August, Faith qualified
for supplemental security income, and we received a retroactive check. The
income was designed to supplement the added expense required by individuals
with disabilities. Quinn and Shale also received back payments, thousands
of dollars worth. Kyle bid several large jobs that were very promising, and
things were finally on the upswing for us.

Over Labor Day, we piled our three children in the car and went on a
vacation. It was the first in a very long time. We visited family we hadn't seen
in years, stayed in a beautiful hotel, enjoyed a spectacular play, and toured a
breathtaking national park. It was magnificent. Though I was still caring for
two children with disabilities, it was a breeze compared to caring for Quinn.
I loved and missed him dearly, but I cherished the break.

Shale returned to preschool a different child. Being so sensitive to loud noises and overstimulation, Quinn's outbursts had been a significant source of stress for him. But now Shale was calm and relaxed and even developed a playful sense of humor. With just the right tone of voice, I could tickle him from across the room. I simply repeated his name in a silly voice, gradually mounting in volume, until finally he erupted in laughter. It was truly charming.

Faith was almost two and began preschool for children with special needs. Now that Quinn was gone, we saw a great improvement in her development. Her animal sounds morphed into words, and she began communicating more effectively. She became engaging and confident, venturing out of my arms more frequently.

Jaede began inviting friends over without fear. Soon giggly little neighborhood girls filled our apartment. It was a thrill to see her actually be a child again. She was finally able to unlock her creativity, unencumbered by her previous limitations. She was excited to have latches come off the doors, gates come down, and to receive more of the one thing she wanted more than anything else: my attention.

Kyle and I actually slept through the night for the first time in a long while. We read, we talked, we laughed, and we even went out in public as a family without making too big of a scene. We were still stared at, but I didn't care. I was so glad to no longer be cooped up in our apartment all day long. Even though I didn't feel like a "normal" mother, I enjoyed this newfound freedom.

The despair I had known just a few months prior seemed far away now, and I gained a confidence about myself that had been missing for a long time. I truly felt beautiful again. I even tapped into a few old friendships and had something of a social life. I became more in tune to inspiration, and abundant gratitude filled me. There was beauty all around me, even in the simplest details like the sky, the moon, and the clouds. I saw the hand of divinity in my life again, and I marveled at how often we take these works of art for granted. But I would acknowledge and even celebrate these beautiful miracles coming to the surface. Even the burdens that had been lifted from my shoulders five months earlier left an indelible imprint on my soul—their lessons, their wisdom, their breath of life. They, too, were gifts.

These realizations were like spiritual pages turning in my life, exposing a parallel world of light and miracles between the lines and revealing the inherent luster that had been hiding under the surface. I had not been forgotten. I was remembered, I was appreciated, and I was loved. There was a merciful God somewhere who knew and understood me. I opened my heart and let the blessings in. Heaven was no longer silent, or maybe the chaos had dissipated enough to enable me to finally hear it again.

Over the months that followed, I put ideas into words and wrote poem after poem. Life was grand in her broad scope, her harsh hammerings, and her graceful wisdom. I set my pen to paper and out flowed truth, light, and power. This personal renaissance was vastly greater than the awakening I had encountered in high school. I wanted to express how I envisioned my disabled children and the world around me. I wanted to make the suffering I had known somehow meaningful.

I stood back and saw a transformation that had taken place. I saw a young, starry-eyed girl with plans and goals that didn't include compassion or courage, trials, or failures, or life lessons. And they certainly didn't include disabled children. I loved this amazing girl for her die-hard idealism and her unconventional originality. I admired her naïve ambition and her lofty dreams. But I saw those dreams shatter, and her idealism crushed by the anvil of reality. I saw a girl become a woman and, by necessity, leave behind her girlish ways. At twenty-eight years old, a strong and wise woman now stood in her place. A new path was set before her, and she bravely took it. It was a road less traveled—a path that would seek to lift and inspire those whose sorrow she had known herself. This journey would require nothing less than the courage and wisdom forged only in life's rarest of adversities.

November 9, 1997

When found I eternal purpose? When proved I my soul's desire? When saw I the face of God? 'Twas in the heat of the Refiner's Fire.

CHAPTER SIXTEEN
Family Anew

Though I sorely needed the break and was cherishing the quiet time, my heart ached for Quinn. My son was only six-and-a-half years old and so vulnerable. We brought him home for visits every other weekend and were so excited to have him with us during that short time, in contrast to the frustration we all felt toward Quinn just months earlier. Now that he was gone, I loved him all the more. I soon forgot about the sea of crumbs, the mountain of diapers, and the river of vomit. Instead, I thought about his infectious laugh and outrageous sense of humor. Quinn's burst of laughter was cause for celebration and a source of joy to my soul. When Quinn knew he wasn't supposed to have something, he snatched it and took off running—laughing the whole time. Nothing would get him going like a good chase. Quinn was master of the chase. He loved to see us exhausted and out of breath. He also laughed at the strangest things, like when someone fell off a bike, or tripped, or met with some other misfortune. Quinn always saw the raw humor in humanity.

Oh, how I missed him.

I loved Quinn with a unique and heart-wrenching love, the kind of love that overflows and drives one crazy with conflict. It was bittersweet, a torturous yearning, and a deep and abiding attachment that haunted me every day he was gone. Though I didn't fully understand it, I felt its presence in the very deepest part of my soul.

* * * * * * *

Christmas approached and, as was always the case around the holidays, there was a lot to think about. Without Quinn around, I was more keenly aware of and affected by everything else in my life. It seemed December was the floodgate for all the memories associated with my mother's parting, and I now saw reminders everywhere I looked—the decorated holiday trees, the glimmering lights, the poignant carols. It felt as though a rift in time opened to that day in 1977, superimposing a layer of the past directly onto my current world.

> *November 14, 1997*
>
> *I figured out that it will be twenty years this December since my mother died. That part of my life seems more real to me now. I realized that my mother was about my age when she developed cancer. For the first time ever, I seriously considered what it would be like if I died. I couldn't imagine leaving behind Kyle and our children. I don't think I'll die young, but these thoughts and feelings have made my mother seem not so far removed. We never know how long we'll be here. Life just seems so frail right now.*

My mind reflected back to the luminous encounter of that night long ago. It all seemed so mysterious—my mother's young, flawless face, her piercing blue eyes, her profound and captivating love.

Are you watching over me still? Do you share in my life's experiences somehow? I wanted to believe so.

It had been years since that day in the backseat of our little car looking through her albums and scrapbooks. Though I wasn't sure what information awaited me, still I felt drawn to learn more about her. My memories were few and isolated, and I hungered for information.

My dad didn't speak of her often. Though it had been decades since my mother's death, his pain was still so raw. When he did mention her, it was always brief and vague. His eyes would mist on those rare occasions when I brought up her name, and we always spoke in hushed tones. It was our sacred little secret.

On one occasion in particular, I was visiting with my dad alone at his house. He cuddled me in his arms, like he had done so many times when I was a little girl, as we sat and reminisced about those far away days. Then he opened up and began sharing things about my mother I had never before heard spoken.

"Your mother was a bit stubborn and head-strong," he began. "We often ran into a battle of wills with each other. I'm telling you, that girl had the will to do whatever she put her mind to. No one could talk Carol out of anything," he chuckled quietly. "She wanted to start a family almost immediately, but I wasn't so sure about that. It scared me. I wasn't ready to be a father. But she had her own plans and, boy, was she persistent," he said. "She really was anxious to be a mother."

He was actually discussing her in detail—something my dad never did—and I listened intently. I didn't know when or if he would ever speak of my mother again.

Remembering, he continued, "Carol had a silly sense of humor. It's one of the things I loved most about her. She'd sit behind the steering wheel of her car with a big lollipop in her mouth, driving down the street like an over-grown kid. It was embarrassing, but she'd just smile and wave as she drove by. She could really laugh at herself. She had quirky little habits that were awfully endearing," he paused. "But she was so proud, so independent . . . ." His voice trailed off wistfully.

I tried to form in my mind's eye an image of this woman my dad was describing. He knew a completely different side of my mother than what I remembered. I recalled the young girl I had seen in her teenage photographs, at the prom, and in her band uniform. I envisioned the light in her eyes and the fun that seemed to exude from her countenance in those youthful pictures. Other images came to mind, too. Ones I didn't want to remember— empty, lost eyes and a strained smile.

"When she became sick, things changed," he went on, gathering his thoughts. "She became more empathetic, more selfless. Her stubborn streak subdued a little, and she told me that we needed to start giving to charity. Even toward the end when she was dying, she talked about how we should help our neighbors and not be selfish with our money. That headstrong girl became very brave in those last two years. She really wanted to live." He paused and then became unusually serious, "She wanted to live, LeeAnn."

I was amazed at my father's words. My mother had apparently experienced a refining process, not unlike mine. It gave me comfort to know that she, too, had been through a fire of her own and had emerged better for it. It even seemed striking that she and I had somewhat parallel experiences. I hadn't seen her transform like my father had, but I did remember toward the end, when the disease had taken hold of her and the physical damage had progressed, she seemed calm, resigned. She seemed to almost surrender.

"She was a good kid," my dad finally said.

* * * * * *

December 30, 1997

Wow, what a big month for us! We have actually moved into a house! It has 3 bedrooms, 2 ½ baths, a 2-car garage, and most importantly a yard. The kids love it here! This has been a dream come true. So much has happened in our short lives together. We are ready now for a season of peace.

We spent the first part of December searching for a rental house that would accommodate our special needs, give us the room we so badly needed, and be a place well-suited for Quinn's return home one day. Within a week, we found a house close by that was everything we were looking for.

We had never lived in a house before, always an apartment or condo. Now we had a yard where the children could run and play, and someplace I could make into a home. As I walked through the rooms, I envisioned how to put my creative talents to work and bring some color back into our environment. My artistic expression had been starved for an outlet, and our new home seemed like the perfect canvas. Functionality had always taken precedence over aesthetics, but with a little extra money I now set to change all that. We bought some new furniture, a few bright accessories, and cheerful curtains for the windows. I even hung pictures. This house would be beautiful, a place Jaede could be proud to bring her friends to and a place where I could entertain guests. Maybe we could begin to feel like a *normal* family, as if we knew what that was.

We bought a trampoline and set it up in the backyard. Soon all the neighborhood kids were over jumping, and Jaede was the cool new girl on the block. She was approaching eight years old and I wanted her to have some part of a normal childhood. I wanted her to blossom into the amazing girl I knew her to be.

Shale had a room to himself until Quinn returned. However, the stairs in our new two-story house posed a problem for him. He couldn't navigate them alone. He walked like a blind man feeling his way with his feet one stair at a time. Though Shale's eye surgery had been successful, his depth perception remained substantially impaired.

Faith was two and slept in a crib in our master bedroom. Her disability had manifested mainly in learning delays and emotional problems. She was unusually sensitive to loud sounds and disturbances, as well. Though she was still somewhat timid, I felt that she, too, would blossom in this new environment.

During this time, I began serving as a youth mentor to a group of teenage girls. I volunteered twice per week in addition to special trips every few months. The girls accepted me with open arms, and I found new purpose. The experience was rewarding, and inspired me deeply. Though I came into the role as a teacher, I soon found they were teaching me.

I was enjoying the peace of our manageable little family and the new opportunities being afforded us. We truly cherished our time together in that beautiful house. Kyle and I graduated from fifty-cent candy bar dates to dinner and a movie. We listened to music with our children, danced around the house, sang songs, and played games. We held themed parties and hosted sleepovers for Jaede and her friends. We took walks every evening, slept through the night most nights, and had family meals together every day. The sound of laughter filled the air, and we had color and beauty and cheer in our home.

> *July 14, 1998*
> *Every once in a while I get a glimpse of how fortunate I am and how rare that is in this world. I am a different person than I was ten years ago. I am learning more and more who I really am and my divine potential. I can see that potential in others as well as myself. Life is a great instructor.*

Our plan was to bring Quinn home in August. We worked closely with our caseworker to qualify for in-home care. We requested a full-time respite provider to work with Quinn eight hours a day with self-care needs such as bathing, feeding, laundry, and dressing. The level of services being offered to us was unprecedented in the agency we were working with. A family with three disabled children was highly unusual. We made arrangements to hire a staff member who was currently working with Quinn at the group home. He had worked with individuals with special needs for years and already knew Quinn's routines and behaviors. Quinn had been in the group home for more than ten months, and we felt prepared, emotionally and physically, for his return.

Kyle scheduled a vasectomy and my relief was immense. With the risk of having another child with Fragile X syndrome, the need was urgent. Finally I would be able to relax without the fear of getting pregnant each month. This was significant in giving me the confidence I would need to manage Quinn and Shale effectively. More than anything, it was a tremendous boon to my morale.

The day we brought Quinn home was a happy and tearful reunion. When we pulled up in front of our house, I felt like we were bringing home a new baby. Quinn was a different child in many ways now. The structured environment of the group home had disciplined him. He was manageable for them. I hoped he would be manageable for me. They had trained him to eat with a spoon and clean up after himself. I hoped he would retain those skills. In the group home, he was happy and well adjusted. I hoped he would be happy here with us. Though I felt a spell of anxiety, I subdued it.

We stood around and watched as Quinn entered the house and explored, apprehensively at first. He soon became excited and began jumping around and giggling. Then, as if to say, *Hey gang, what are you waiting for? The fun has returned!* He burst into the wildest laughter—that familiar hearty laugh that I had missed so much while he was away. It wasn't long before we were all laughing, crowding around him in a great big sloppy, goose-fleshed group hug.

Quinn was home. My baby was finally home.

CHAPTER SEVENTEEN
Pathway to Dawn

Though our home was already childproofed for Shale and Faith, it was time to Quinn-proof it. Down came all the pictures on the walls and accessories on the shelves. We installed a solid wood gate in the kitchen—latched on the inside so he couldn't reach it, changed out all the doorknobs to locking, and installed a double-sided dead bolt on our front door which could only be opened with a key. Though Quinn had learned how to feed himself, communicate his needs better through gestures, and cooperate during baths and dressing, he was still non-verbal and hadn't been toilet trained. I had three in diapers again.

Quinn was accustomed to a strictly structured environment at the group home, but at our house, even with the new caregiver, there was only so much we could do. Quinn enjoyed his new freedoms a little too much, and an entirely new noise level emerged. He and Shale reverted to their growling competitions again, and unfortunately, Faith joined in, too. Jaede was a little self-conscious about bringing her friends around now that Quinn was back. Our home went from a peaceful, manageable environment to organized chaos literally overnight, and our newfound flexibility and freedoms virtually vanished.

It was at this time that I made an unthinkable discovery: I was pregnant. I had evidently conceived just before Kyle's vasectomy. The irony was devastating.

Why is this happening? I demanded. *How can I possibly do this again?*

The idea of having another baby now was staggering. I was at my limit, barely able to manage the children I already had. I couldn't begin to imagine bringing a new baby into our situation. And, if we had another one like Quinn or Shale . . . the thought paralyzed me.

Please, Mom. Please help me . . .

I was losing ground, back at square one, and I sensed the foundation shifting under my feet again.

* * * * * * *

In January, a ray of hope was shed. Jaede was tested for Fragile X syndrome to rule out the possibility she might be a carrier of the genetic disorder. Incredibly, she did not even carry the gene. We were ecstatic. I wanted her to one day leave home and lead a normal life, away from the stresses of our current circumstance and without disabled children of her own. With these test results came significant hope for Jaede's future.

My little sister was also tested at this time, and it was determined that she did not carry the gene. Though she continued to struggle emotionally, with these test results, she, too, would be free to move forward without a genetic disability to impede her.

With the uncertainty of my unborn child's future looming, and perhaps with some divine nudging, I delved deeper into the universe that surrounded me—my disabled children and their unique community. I was searching for answers, reaching into the darkness for anything that could illuminate this painfully dynamic and ever-changing sphere. With Faith in adaptive preschool and both Quinn and Shale in special education programs, I was fully entrenched now in the community of special needs. My heart was changing, evolving further and deeper despite—or perhaps because of— the weight of my circumstances. A hidden side of this universe was calling me, drawing my spirit into an understanding that surpassed everything I had experienced up to that point. And it opened me up to something all-encompassing and surprisingly beautiful.

I discovered the most amazing people in this unique community. These were people unencumbered by the pressures of status or social conformity, individuals who stood separate and apart from the rest of the world. The special education teachers, classroom aids, caseworkers, respite care providers, parents and siblings of disabled children, speech-occupational-physical therapists, behavioral specialists, and even the bus drivers who drove my children to school each day were all extraordinary.

These unique individuals worked daily with the disabled, witnessing their suffering first hand. They willingly selected to do a work most people would never do, changing diapers on full-grown children, watching seizures happen, communicating without the luxury of verbal language, and often managing extreme behaviors. Theirs was a universe of silence and struggle, a world of triumph over insurmountable odds and victory over inescapable obstacles. With a love pure and undefiled, these selfless caregivers were like angels incarnate.

Both the parents and professionals in this community were pristinely compassionate souls I confided in regarding the pain of mothering children with special needs. Their hearts were laid bare; there was no pretense or ego among them. I realized how smug and falsely sincere others had been in my life, putting on an air of self-importance just to impress me. How silly it all seemed now. How pathetic. It opened my eyes to how shallow and narrow-minded people can be. And it humbled me to know that perhaps I, too, had once been shallow and narrow-minded. But now I was part of this community whose members were a breath of fresh air in a suffocating world—living, breathing men and women on a planet filled with those sleepwalking through life. Indeed, they were extraordinary individuals in a world of the ordinary. And though I had been involuntarily—even painfully—drafted into it, I counted myself privileged to be numbered among them.

I began realizing that children with disabilities were strangely gifted. Not that they were reading above grade-level or competing for trophies. They didn't have record-breaking test scores or inflated IQs. In fact, they were made fun of, avoided on the playground, mocked with rude gestures, and called "retards." Their facial features were often deformed or misshapen, their bodies awkward and broken. Their speech—if they had any at all—was muddled and incoherent, and many of them lived out their lives confined to a wheelchair. Even the educators who worked with them were often ostracized by other faculty members. It was true that these special children were the ones no one wanted to be like. They went to bed every night and awoke every morning with the same devastating challenge. Yet they were courageous and amazing and were the bearers of a profound gift: the ability to humble even the most arrogant person, to awaken the most conceited, self-centered mind to what is real. It was the gift of opening the eyes of the blinded individual and making them see, opening the ears of the deafened soul and making them hear. It was the essence of brazen heroism in a world of fear and cowardice. The powerful aptitude for capturing in a single glance the very epitome of suffering and making it impossible to ignore. And it was the rare and unspeakable gift of making visible the face of God.

This wasn't the flawless face of God I had been conditioned to see. This face would not be found in our synagogues or temples, in our churches or cathedrals. We wouldn't read about it in our textbooks or see it represented in our statues or iconic paintings. It wasn't the glorious face of God evidenced in our towering mountaintops or the cosmic mysteries of space, the mighty image of Him in the sunrise or the sunset, the moon or the stars. Nor was it the all-powerful face spoken of from the pulpits or altars of our houses of worship. This was an entirely different side of God, a much less glamorous side. It was vulnerable, shattered, and frail. It inhabited pain and sorrow. It was His glory made manifest in the imperfections as well as the perfections, in the broken as well as the whole, the darkness as well as the light. It was His face hidden in the lowly and deformed, veiled in the weak and rejected. Like the beauty of a rose concealed in its thorns, His face was all the more striking when laid against the backdrop of an uncommon innocence, obscured within a tattered body. He wanted me to recognize Him everywhere, not just in the form of His grand creations, not only in the glaring awe of His great works. He wanted me to find the fathomless light of His face camouflaged in the fragile.

And it was this fragile face of God that I witnessed in my own children.

I learned more about God from Quinn and Shale and Faith than from all my years in Sunday school. They were like open vessels of humility, purity, and revealed mystery in my presence. I found God in the eyes of my disabled children more plainly than in any artistic rendering of Him I had ever seen. Like looking through pools of light, I felt as though I peered into the infinite truths of the cosmos when looking deeply into their eyes. I was taught His precepts more clearly from their painful lessons than from all of my religious instruction combined. Selflessness, innocence, simplicity, and sacrifice—all flowing organically from them in every moment, as though they could be nothing else. My tattered children were indeed the wise teachers, and I was a mere student.

These lessons washed over me fully and irreversibly, driven by an awareness born of first-hand experience. Every point in my life had led up to this learning. Every moment and every event served as a luminous building block that prepared me to see and hear and feel—like a rite of passage into an exquisite new understanding. I began to notice Him everywhere, in the imperfections all around me. He had been there all along, if I had but known where to look. He had been there in both the shadow of my mother's death and the luminance of her heavenly visit. He had been there in the consuming blaze of the refiner's fire and in the triumphant miracle of our emergence. In both the darkness that veiled my children's eyes and the brightness of their pristine innocence, He had shown himself. He wanted to reveal to me who He was, who He has always been, if I was willing to open my heart to it. He wanted me to never doubt His existence because of frailties and sufferings, but to understand ever so gently that it is there where we will find Him. He wanted me to look past the diapers and the vomit and the tantrums and see His face, there in the light of my children's eyes. In Quinn and Shale and Faith, He was unencumbered. In them, His mysteries were made plain. In them, He became visible.

Through the dense shadow of the place I inhabited came the starlit presence of divine power. It had been in the beauty and perfection where I had always sought it, but it was in the chaos and the darkness where I finally found it.

Like a strange dichotomy of triumph and tragedy, God existed in them both simultaneously—something I would have never supposed. Any notions I previously held about perfection were all at once obsolete, and I saw that perhaps it wasn't the world around me that was imperfect, but my definition of it. Both sides of these two opposing forces were so real and vivid, like a larger-than-life paradox manifesting itself all around me. Though in constant contradiction to one another, they compatibly coexisted in a multi-faceted and beautiful enigma. The love and hate, joy and bitterness; I passed between them both on a daily, even hourly, basis, as I struggled to understand the nature of my children and their afflictions. Evidences of this concept weaved itself through the story of my life like an unbreakable thread, revealing itself in various moments and evolving in my understanding to it. I discovered the very paradox within myself: my conflict between loving my children while at the same time despairing over them; simultaneously feeling love from God and betrayal by Him for giving me such heavy hardships. In the culmination of everything I had experienced up to that time, I saw how this mysterious juxtaposition affected my entire life, even the whole human experience. And I saw how the fragile face of God informs our world.

We were not random beings flung together on a sphere of clay only to lapse into error and be ostracized by heaven's love. Nor were we mindless souls adrift without purpose on a sea of hopeless outcomes. Life held more, so much more, for all of us, and this was only the beginning to understanding how it all fit together. My special children were just one example of the fragile personified, and I began to see, to my surprise, what a profound effect they were having on a great many others as the scope of their influence transcended the walls of our home. Family, friends, and care providers referred to my children as "unforgettable" and "inspiring." Tears flowed from their eyes as they spoke of the sacred and endearing qualities embodied in Quinn, Shale, and Faith. They may have been a tremendous challenge, but these children left an indelible impression on all who came in contact with them.

Like the strange teenage girl at the mall whom my mother labeled "handicapped" and the young man with Down Syndrome who told me he loved me, all of these uncommon souls had crossed my path, and not one of them had been forgotten. They had all caused me to slow down and become aware, beckoning me to view the world through a different set of eyes, to experience the present more fully, to see life as it truly was and things as they truly are. As my unique experiences chipped away at the external world around me, I began to notice the things of the spirit more clearly. Through the darkness I had come, and was now in the embrace of a fully transformative dawn breaking across the horizon of my despair.

As I freed my tethered self, I realized there was so much wonder and awe around me. My world was being stripped away one painful piece at a time, but I was connecting to another world that had been previously cloaked. I finally understood that it is often through profound deprivation that one begins to see what truly matters, to feel the sublime glow of love, and to sense the existence of God. The veil separating us and eternity grows thinner, and it is then that we begin to discover our divine nature.

What will I do with the knowledge I have been given? What will I do with the experiences I have lived? I had been admitted into an exclusive club whose members were easily identified by their physical and cognitive deficits and whose mantra was to never give up. I had been accepted into an elite company of amazing people who depended on one another for support and advocacy in a world racked with ignorance and intolerance. I had been embraced by the very individuals whose unconditional love was changing the world. *Can I love without condition? Can I be courageous and even heroic like the handicapped children whose name I bear?* I held within me the power to never give up, the ability to support and advocate. *Will I use that power?* I had been entrusted with the sacred privilege of seeing the soul in its purest form through the penetrating eyes of my young children. *Will I never forget?*

This new understanding became a gateway to another possibility, an idea that crept gracefully into my mind and took root there. I began to perceive disabled children as valiant angels who sought to come into mortality for the express purpose of helping and teaching others. They wouldn't be equipped with the standard intelligence or physical capacity of their peers, nor would they be pretty to look at or necessarily fun to be with. They wouldn't be born of privilege or enjoy a life of ease. Rather, theirs would be an existence of struggle and hardship and sorrow—a life of suffering from which there would be no escape. They would be well acquainted with pain in all its cruelest forms. And they would know the darkness intimately. But perhaps the allure of comfort and worldly success didn't appeal to them. Instead, they may have been more interested in what difference they could make for good among the human race. Perhaps they knowingly relinquished any opportunity for healing, choosing instead to heal the prideful and blinded species that humanity was in danger of becoming. They may have felt that a lifetime of suffering was a small price to pay for the priceless opportunity of teaching compassion and humility to us all. Maybe they realized that this was the only way.

I imagined they knew full well the challenges they would face, the heartache they would feel, and the burden they would be on society. I bet they had full disclosure. But in the interest of saving a race immersed in anger and corruption, they put themselves in a position of pure love and selflessness. It was a cause and they enlisted, willingly opting to serve their fellow man as a reminder that there is still time to be happy and there is every reason to be grateful. Maybe they wanted to be living proof that we don't need words to communicate, we don't need beauty to be beautiful, and we don't need intelligence to be wise. Quite possibly they chose their affliction in a moment when they could see the whole picture clearly and were brave enough and strong enough to come here and help the rest of us in the slim chance that we would not turn away from them and stay in our ignorance. Maybe, just maybe, they felt it would be worth it.

It was through this illuminating perspective that I saw my own children. In the curious instances when Shale tilted his head upside down to smile and peer deeply into my eyes, I knew he was communicating in a language all his own. I even joked that God had put his eyeballs in upside down. In the rare occasions when Quinn pressed his lips to my face in his version of a kiss, I knew he somehow loved me and appreciated all I did for him. Sometimes he made a whisper that sounded an awful lot like "ma" if I let myself believe it. In the precious embrace of Faith's delicate hug and the light behind her eyes, I knew *exactly* who she was. She had an important work to do here in this life, if I would just be patient enough to help her do it.

My entire universe was recreating itself, compelled by the faces that surrounded me every day—the disabled and those who cared for them, the frail and the flawless, the fragile and the majestic. Existing at both ends of the spectrum simultaneously, in the two opposing realities that comprised my life, I found meaning. This universe was brightly stunning, vividly colorful, and deeply moving. It was also pain and loss made larger than life, and it had my name written all over it in bold letters. In this universe, opposition had purpose and sorrow gave rise to miracles. I had proof in the imperfect children and the lessons they were teaching me. Only after the darkness had been fully manifested in my life could the fullness of the Light be revealed.

All of these realizations came rising up into my world, bursting like blossoms through the rain-soaked earth after a storm. Redefining for a scared little girl the awkward and strange into the sacred and beautiful. Renewing a naïve young woman's idea of what is truly important. And creating luminous moments when all other insignificant things fall away, leaving behind only what is true and real.

It was in this world of bittersweet beauty and rare reckoning that I lived.

Chapter Eighteen
Gifts for Hearts That Long

My due date was fast approaching. I carried on with tending to my children and going about my tasks with the usual vigor. The impact of the pregnancy was so minimal that I hardly noticed my body was in the major process of creating a living being. However, my heightened spiritual sense continued throughout the duration, opening my eyes and my heart even further to the sprawling Light emerging across my horizon.

I wrote in my journal less frequently after Quinn returned home, and my season of poetry ended. However, my mentoring continued. It was very fulfilling and allowed me a forum where I could be the unconventional, enthusiastic young woman I had been before my marriage. Mentoring gave me motivation outside the diapers, pregnancy, and disabilities.

In preparation for our baby's arrival, I wanted to choose a name that was unique and very distinctive. Though my heart longed for a non-disabled child, I knew the odds were not in favor of this desire. I decided that this name would be a symbol of new hope. In it lay so much promise.

One night, I was lying in bed thinking about possible baby names. The children were asleep, and Kyle sat a few feet away at his computer playing games, something he had begun doing frequently. With Quinn reassuming his difficult behaviors and the impending arrival of our new baby, the stress had compounded. A hectic life had resumed in the last few months, and the pregnancy had just sort of passed by. Only a month remained before my due date, and Kyle and I had not taken much time to talk. I felt pressed to make a decision on a name. That night seemed like the perfect opportunity.

I propped up my head on the pillow and asked, "What do you think about a name for the baby? Any suggestions?"

His eyes remained glued to the screen.

"I have some ideas. Can we talk about them?" I continued, hoping to evoke a response.

He didn't say a word, but he kept on playing like I wasn't there.

"We only have a month before the baby comes."

Nothing.

I laid my head back down and stared up at the ceiling. *It's no use,* I thought. My heart ached from the lack of attention. I pulled the covers up over my head and secretly wept.

There were days when I felt as if I, alone, carried our relationship, while Kyle gravitated toward things such as social experiences, television, or computer games. He seemed to have lost touch with who I was and what was important to me. The few times I shared comments about my personal interests, he only gave me a courteous smile and stock response so we could get right back to talking about him again. Our relationship had been like this for so long, I was used to it. But as our situation grew more demanding, Kyle grew more distant. I felt the weight grow larger and the obligation more substantial, giving all of my time and energy to it. Though I didn't know exactly what the future held, I knew I didn't want to face it alone. *You say you love me,* I wanted to tell him, *but do you know what love is?* I had experienced it firsthand in an all-consuming encounter full of power and light—and boundless hope. I longed for that hope now. I longed to be embraced by someone who loved me fully and who regarded me with the transformative cherishing I had once known.

I had no inkling yet of the true love that would soon be mine, the cherishing that awaited me, nor the heavy price that would be exacted of me to pay for it.

April 22, 1999
A new arrival has blessed our home! Psalm was born Friday, April 16!
She is a cute, blonde, petite young lady. We are so grateful to have this
little girl. How strange to think that she almost didn't come, as we had
decided not to have more children. I chose her name for what it means:
a sacred song or poem. That fits her perfectly.

The name I chose for my new daughter, Psalm, was a symbol of the hope I held close to my heart, the sacred wish for a happier life, lending her birth an infusion of new possibilities. Psalm was extraordinary and absolutely beautiful. As Kyle and I pulled into the garage with her for the first time, everyone was there—our children, our caregiver, my stepmom, and all the neighborhood kids. We were an anomaly in our 2.5-kid, white-picket-fenced neighborhood, and everyone wanted a peek.

I brought the new bundle into our living room and sat down on the couch. Everyone crowded in over my shoulder—oohing and aahing—eager to take a look at the newest member of our unusual family. I gently pulled back her wrap to reveal a lock of wispy, blond hair and a patch of flawless ivory skin. Two small blue eyes peeked out from under the blanket.

I wasn't sure what everyone expected Psalm would be like, but I knew what was on everyone's mind. The unspoken fear that lay silent behind their eyes. She was as perfect as could be, a tiny girl wrapped in a pink blanket. None of us knew whether or not she carried the defective gene that had severely disabled her three older siblings. And nobody dared mention it.

Psalm's presence was pure joy. I cherished every moment with her, staring at her perfect little features and giving thanks for this unexpected but awesome opportunity. How grateful I was for the privilege to love and adore her. No matter what her future held and regardless of whether or not she had any kind of disability, I loved her fully and infinitely. The spirit that lay behind her eyes was the real Psalm, despite any potential flaw in her genes, and that was who I would love forever.

We set up Psalm's crib in our master bedroom, which now served as the nursery, Kyle's office, and Shale's sleeping quarters. Jaede proved to be a tremendous help during this time, holding Psalm while I changed diapers or gave baths to the other children. She also learned to do laundry and prepare food, displaying a level of maturity uncommon for her nine years of age.

Unlike most children who dream of doing grown-up things, Jaede was a little grown-up who dreamt of doing childlike things. She spent most of her free time playing outside in the large tree in our neighborhood where she found a peaceful escape she called "Jaede's world." It was a place of daydreams and enchantment, free from the constant anxiety of our home life and the challenges of her siblings. Her inability to concentrate during schoolwork and her difficulty sleeping were all symptoms of the stress levels typical in our household. But she jettisoned away often to this whimsical retreat in the branches where she could dream of playhouses and art classes and violin lessons—all the things Jaede longed for but could not have. Deep into the bark was her name carved over and over, up and around the trunk and into the towering limbs. Jaede, Jaede, Jaede, Jaede, a little girl with a heart the size of earth just waiting to be set free.

* * * * * *

In order to prepare for our new life with Psalm, and due to the importance of early intervention, we wasted no time in having her tested. Because we already had three children with Fragile X syndrome, our new baby qualified for the screening. At two weeks old, we had Psalm's blood drawn and the genetic screening done. The first blood sample became compromised, however, so we took her in to have another sample drawn and began the waiting process all over again.

While waiting for Psalm's test results, I watched her development closely. Those test results would determine her course in life, and I had an enormous amount of emotion invested in them. I called weekly to the geneticist to check the status. Months went by and still no word.

The day the phone call finally came, I was home alone with Faith and Psalm. I stood in the kitchen holding tight to the phone. Time seemed to stand still. I looked over at Psalm sitting in her baby seat and felt the weight of the news I was about to receive. She would be a blessing in my life no matter what the results were, but I also realized that in this moment our lives would be forever changed.

The doctor spoke briefly.

"Are you sure?" I gasped.

"I'm sure," she replied.

I was speechless.

> *November 17, 1999*
>
> *Today is a joyous day for us. This morning I received the best news I could possibly hope for. My baby, Psalm, does not have the Fragile X gene! She is not even a carrier! I can hardly believe it! It has been so long since I've had a "typical" baby, I hardly know what to do! My relief is inexpressible. We have been given a gift this day. I will never forget it.*

Tears flowed freely as I grabbed Psalm and held her close to my heart. I immediately called Kyle at work to give him the good news.

"Psalm is not disabled!" It felt so good to say those words out loud.

"That's great news," he replied in a way that sounded more like courtesy than excitement.

"Can you believe it?!" I choked out, barely able to contain my relief.

But Kyle was busy, and I didn't want anything to dampen this moment. So I said good-bye and phoned my parents. I knew they anxiously awaited the news. When Isabel answered, I asked them both to get on the phone.

"Psalm is not disabled!" I squealed through my tears. It felt even better to say it a second time.

My parents had been there with me in the heat of the fire. They had witnessed my lowest moments. They knew the stakes. And they now wept openly as I recounted for them what the doctor had told me. Faith was sitting beside me, and soon she began crying, too. Though she was only four years old and didn't know what was happening, she saw my tearful excitement and responded in the only way she knew how.

I had hoped my new baby wouldn't be disabled, but I had not dared believe it. I had been so deeply immersed in this world of therapies and caseworkers and genetic disorders for so long, I had forgotten that typical, healthy children are born every day. Here she was in my arms, a precious daughter, unaware of the enormous miracle she was and of the boundless gratitude overflowing my heart in that moment.

"It's so wonderful, so wonderful, so wonderful," I cried over and over.

"So wunnaful, so wunnaful, so wunnaful," repeated Faith through her tears.

And it was . . . so wonderful.

* * * * * * *

Life with Psalm was bliss. It had been nine years since I had a baby without a disability. I felt like a new mom in some ways. Psalm smiled at me, played with toys appropriately, laughed, cooed, and cuddled. There would be no watching her for strange behaviors or developmental delays, and no worried nights lying awake. I put all thoughts of early intervention therapy out of my mind completely, and I just marveled. The horror of my unexpected pregnancy had transformed into the most amazing blessing of Psalm's presence in my life. It was yet another example of that divine dichotomy that kept showing up. A despairing experience made beautiful. It was the near-impossible occurring effortlessly, with graceful ease. I stood in awe at the power of this defining theme throughout my life, at the breadth in which

I had experienced both the sweetest and the most bitter of moments. And I dearly savored the sweetness of the moment at hand.

One afternoon as I was working with Faith on her speech therapy, going through each family member's name, she surprised me.

"My brother is an angel."

Faith had no concept of what an angel was or the vocabulary to express it.

"Your brother is Quinn," I responded.

"Quinn is an angel," she stated again.

"And Shale is your brother, too," I said. Now I was testing her, remembering back to the day when Jaede had said the very same thing about Quinn.

"Shale is an angel," she replied.

My heart skipped a beat.

Shortly after this experience, I walked in on Quinn one night and found him sitting in the middle of his bedroom floor in the dark. The light from the hall illuminated his countenance and I noticed he was staring up at the ceiling, smiling. I stopped in the doorway to watch. He sat perfectly still, aglow with the most serene expression I had ever witnessed on him. I glanced to where his gaze was focused on the corner of the ceiling, but saw nothing. Yet he was transfixed. Though I stood a few mere feet away, he didn't even notice me. It was as if I were witnessing an exchange between Quinn and a heavenly visitor. A peaceful warmth washed over me. After a moment, I stepped quietly back and closed his door.

A distinct sense of otherworldly presence permeated our home, and our children were the conduit. So innocent and pure, their eyes were a window into another realm, albeit distant, and a doorway to the divine. Despite their odd and often destructive behaviors, I knew my special children were close to heaven, and heaven was close to them. These experiences made me long for my mother's spirit, and I wished that she was present in the lives of her grandchildren.

January 1, 2000

Happy New Year—new decade, new century, new millennium! Wow, what a date! There are fireworks going on outside. All is quiet in our home. Only Kyle and I are awake. I hope the next millennium dawns a brighter day . . . What will the future hold? Will we be ready?

PART FOUR

Edge of the Cliff

CHAPTER NINETEEN
Falling by Degrees

The following summer, I made the decision to home school Jaede. She had struggled in her studies the year before and had fallen behind. She needed one-on-one support, something I hadn't been able to give her. While Psalm napped and my other children were in school, Jaede and I worked together and grew closer than we had ever been. In the process, this bright-eyed, wise-beyond-her-years little lady became my dearest friend.

Meanwhile, change was in the air.

August 8, 2000

A week or so ago I started thinking about moving—far away. This is a thought that has been out of the question for me before. At first, I casually mentioned this idea to Kyle. Now he and Jaede are totally excited about it. It seems our initial search has narrowed down to the Salt Lake area, in Utah. Isn't that strange? A month ago, I would have laughed at the idea. The future may be finding us abroad.

The idea to move out of state came unexpectedly into my heart. Though I had always been a California girl, I now turned my thoughts to starting over someplace new. I was ready for a drastic change. This thought took hold suddenly and almost urgently. However, it was much more than just a thought. It was a *longing*.

Plans and arrangements for our move occupied the majority of that year. We learned that Salt Lake City had an excellent school for children with disabilities. In addition, we could buy land there and build our own home for less than we could buy an existing house in California. Building a custom home designed specifically for our family's special needs was highly appealing to me, and I soon became the catalyst that was now driving us forward. I wanted a new start someplace completely different. I wanted to be someplace where no one knew us.

The novelty of Quinn's return had worn off quickly. With my time being divided among five children, Quinn fought for attention like never before. His tolerance levels dropped dramatically while his tantrums skyrocketed. He was confident and unruly and took control of our household. He seemed to have lost all the skills he learned at the group home and adopted a more destructive, troublesome disposition. In combination with Shale's and Faith's growing difficulties, the situation was escalating out of control.

An alarming myriad of problems related to my children's disorder surfaced. In addition to Fragile X syndrome, Quinn was also diagnosed with ADHD, mood disorder/bi-polar spectrum, and anxiety disorder. Shale had a form of Tourette's syndrome, manifesting in uncontrollable outbursts and spasms. Faith had severe anxiety issues. And all three of them had autism. Communicating with Quinn or Shale was a challenge. We tried a picture communication system where they could choose the item they wanted from a group of basic pictures, but they never caught on to it. All three suffered from emotional disturbances as well. They were greatly affected by their environment and by the moods of those around them. They seemed highly perceptive to *my* mood in particular, especially if I was stressed.

Since Quinn was a toddler, he had been fascinated with his feces, but he was beginning to seek out this sensory stimulation more frequently. This repulsed me. The more I worked to clean it up, the more I came in contact with it. One time when Quinn's caregiver was late for work, Quinn managed to wipe feces on the walls leading all the way up the stairs before he was caught. In addition to the disgusting mess, this also presented a potentially serious health risk. Children with hygienic issues often carry dangerous bacteria with them.

Clothes were constantly filthy, making laundry a seriously dirty job. Both Quinn and Shale went through several outfits each day. Everything they touched was contaminated, including me. I looked gross and felt gross nearly all the time. I often found vomit or feces under their fingernails or in their hair, but clipping nails and cutting hair was a torturous ordeal. They screamed and muscled until I couldn't hold them still. I feared the neighbors would hear their cries of agony and think we were beating them. It was an emotionally traumatic experience.

Each of them also had a highly sensitive gag reflex and digestive disorders which resulted in vomiting and an unusually high volume of bowel movements. Though they ate continuously throughout the day, they seemed ravenous all the time and were extremely thin. That Fragile X metabolism was enviable. Quinn and Shale also displayed pica, a behavior that caused them to put inedible objects into their mouths seeking oral stimulation. Quinn had once bitten into a rock, breaking his back tooth into shards and shredding his gums, filling his entire mouth with blood.

Poor muscle tone and connective tissue disorder made their limbs like rubber, although when they were angry they seemed unusually strong. Their hyper-flexed joints created a very distinctive appearance and each of them moved their hands and fingers in strange positions, often severely bending or flexing them. As they grew older, unusual facial features became apparent, especially in Quinn and Shale. Their ears grew abnormally large and their faces became elongated.

Though I knew the sweet innocence of their spirits, I also knew they were becoming more than I could manage. They were completely dependent on me for everything, including keeping them safe from harm. Our current neighborhood was in close proximity to a major intersection and posed a serious threat. They had no sense of safety and often took off running. One day Quinn made it all the way to the intersection. I wondered how many people saw a grown boy in a diaper running down the street without thinking to try to stop him. A motorist who happened to be driving by figured he was lost and picked him up. But when the man tried to ask him where he lived, Quinn only growled. Because Quinn and Shale were nonverbal, I had them wear identification bracelets with our contact information on them. But this man didn't think to check. Kyle, Jaede, and I ran down the street frantically searching every yard, calling out Quinn's name in the unlikely chance he would respond to it. Then a neighbor pointed in the direction of the intersection. I was terrified. We rushed around the corner and spotted the motorist who had picked Quinn up. He promptly drove him over to us, but it scared me that my son would get into a car with a complete stranger. I realized then the mounting danger my children faced.

Life became unmanageable. I found myself unable to control my sons and fearing for the safety of my daughters. One morning as I was cleaning the house, Shale pushed Faith down a half flight of stairs. I jumped down the stairs to grab my three-and-a-half-year-old daughter, checking her for injuries. Remarkably she was alright, but I began to see Quinn and Shale as potential threats to their siblings.

They had no concept of boundaries. My once-lovely home was now in shambles. They tore down the curtains, threw my vases against the brick hearth, and emptied the fireplace of the soot. We replaced our sofa every two months at the local thrift store. Gradually our house became a bare skeleton of empty rooms. At Christmas time, our tree grew more and more sparse. Ornaments presented too much temptation for the children; they played with them like toys, pulling them off the tree and often breaking them. They even pulled the tree over onto themselves a number of times. When I found Quinn juggling the heads of two wise men on our dining table, I permanently packed away what was left of our porcelain nativity set.

The most intense challenge came over winter break when our children were out of school for two weeks. Our caregiver took time off, leaving me to tend alone. And though I braced myself for it, I was not prepared. After being cooped up in the house all day, Quinn grew extremely frustrated. He had a fiery temper, and, at nine years old, he was stronger than I was. With an adrenaline rush, he was virtually unstoppable.

On this particular day, Kyle was at work while I tackled the layers of mess built up over days of winter vacation. I kept the windows closed to protect neighbors from our children's noisy outbursts, and the house was extraordinarily stuffy. By noon, I was already exhausted. Quinn clamored at the kitchen gate for more food even though he had eaten four times already that day. A sing-along video pounded from the television while Faith and Psalm played on the floor, toys strewn everywhere. Jaede hung out on a beanbag, and Shale lingered in the next room, purposely distancing himself from Quinn's increasing agitation.

Quinn grabbed my wrist and pulled me to the kitchen gate. He wanted food, and he wanted it fast. I jerked my hand away and told him no; mounds of laundry awaited me upstairs. No sooner had I turned away, when he lashed out at me, scratching my back with his sharp fingernails. I jerked around, red in the face. Quinn saw my anger and yelled out in protest. In the next room, Shale began groaning louder and louder, nervously rocking back and forth. His anxiety was at dangerously high levels. I turned and started for the stairs again, trying to stay calm. I only made it half way up when Quinn lost it. He let out a violent scream and began crying furiously. I ran downstairs to calm him, but he grabbed my hair with both hands and yanked it as hard as he could. I shrieked, wrapping my hands around my head to free myself from Quinn's death grip.

"Quinn, leave me alone!" I shouted. But he came after me again, clawing me fiercely.

Faith and Psalm stared, frozen with fear.

"Stop hurting mom!" Jaede shouted, jumping up to protect me.

"Get away!" I yelled to her, "You'll get hurt!"

I knew that if Quinn didn't get to me, he would go after his siblings, and that would be worse. So I let him take out his anger on me. He grabbed my arms, yanking the skin hard—like a pinch with a vengeance. I screamed at him, ordering him to stop hurting me. I had heard about the unusually high incidence of child abuse among children with special needs, but I wondered about the incidence of parent abuse. Quinn scared me. Shortly after his return, we had tried behavior specialists, behavior classes, and medication, but still he attacked. I had to fight back. I tried to block Quinn's lashings, but he was livid.

"Mom, you have to do something!" Jaede shouted, crying. Instinctively, she grabbed Faith and Psalm and ran them upstairs where they would be safe.

Shale began screaming. Seconds later, he came barreling into the room—both arms forward like a battering ram. He side-swiped me to the floor. I didn't know what hit me. I straightened back up and quickly tried to regain my footing. Shale was too intimidated by Quinn, so he took out his anger on me. He lunged at me, pulling my hair, and then grabbed my arm and dug his nails in. He was in a desperate panic.

Quinn assaulted me from one side while Shale pulled my hair and wailed in agony on the other side. Tears streamed down my face as I struggled to keep them both at arm's length. They were mere children, and I was terrified. Dark thoughts confronted me about what might happen if I lost control. I had never had a temper before, but my sons were trying every last ounce of my patience.

I took hold of Quinn and turned him around backwards, firmly pressing his arms to his sides to restrain him. Carefully I guided him to the kitchen, hoping he would calm down once he was in there. Shale came after me from behind, but I kept walking. Once inside the kitchen, I quickly locked the gate. I was safe from Shale. Quinn heaved and panted, sweating and tear-stained. I took out a box of crackers and tore it open. Quinn snatched it from my hands and shoved a handful into his mouth. The ordeal was over.

Similar episodes occurred many times that year, often while Kyle was away at work, leaving me to manage these frightening tantrums alone. I began to dread each day, awakening every morning with a knot in my stomach. I feared facing Quinn and Shale and I resented having to fight them off. I loved and cherished them, but they brought out the worst in me. I was being pushed over the edge. I felt as if I had done something to warrant their punishment. I didn't understand why they would make their own mother the object of their anger. After sacrificing everything in my life to care for them, it felt like a slap in the face. But still the attacks continued.

I worried about the emotional wellbeing of my daughters who witnessed these treacherous battles on an almost-daily basis. I looked like a madwoman trying to manage my sons, and they looked like lunatics attacking me. I felt so conflicted. I couldn't reconcile the purity of my children's innocence with the cruelty of their behavior. It seemed all wrong. Every story I had heard from fellow parents of disabled children did not compare to what I was experiencing.

Feelings of guilt crept back in and grew almost unbearable. I felt the guilt of knowing I was letting down everyone who looked up to me and my family, the guilt of falling so short of the strong woman I believed myself to be, the guilt of failing at the most important stewardship I would ever have, and the guilt of losing my temper with two blameless handicapped children.

I had seen angelic qualities in Quinn and Shale, signs of a rare and beautiful purity. I knew they were supremely innocent—bearers of a terrible disability which afflicted them. I knew they must have been noble souls—I believed it with all of my heart. They were my sons and I adored them infinitely, yet I began to feel a surge of resentment so deep and suffocating it seemed to engulf me. The more frequent their attacks, the stronger my inner conflict. I was alarmed by what was happening to me. And above all, I couldn't tell a soul.

It was a strange dichotomy—like being simultaneously in both heaven and hell. The face of God froze ablaze in my sons' countenances, like icy infernos staring me straight in the eye, daring me to question it, quickening and flaring with every stroke and assault against me. Day after day it wore on me, piercing my skin and my soul. And every bite, every scratch, was like a knife in my back. It felt intentional.

In those moments, I began to feel something more frightening than anything else up to that point: I hated my sons. They were monsters, both of them, and I resented them for making me a monster, screaming obscenities at them and cursing God for putting me in this horrific situation. We were monsters, each of us. And I hated us all.

It was then I began praying that my sons would be protected from me.

CHAPTER TWENTY

No Longer My Own

Rather than struggle behind closed doors, Kyle and I struggled behind cheerful faces. We had beaten the grim statistics that couples with disabled children face—an eighty-percent divorce rate. We were the ultimate success story and everyone looked up to us.

"You must be amazing people to do what you do," we were frequently told.

But every compliment felt somehow awkward. There was nothing amazing about the way I handled my children. My sons seemed to resent me as much as I resented them. There was no magic in our home, no secret to our success. We merely survived—that was our secret.

In public, our family was a complete spectacle. To go anywhere, Kyle, Jaede, and I each had to push an adaptive stroller for Quinn, Shale, and Faith, while Psalm sat in a baby carrier over my shoulder. I abhorred being stared at. Sometimes people were openly rude, saying things like, "Can't you keep them quiet?" or "What's wrong with them?"

It was hurtful, and it pushed my resentment deeper. I envied mothers who had manageable children with quiet temperaments. They weren't covered in vomit or wearing an adult diaper like mine were. Their children didn't eat rocks or steal other people's food. It seemed unreal to me that mothers could take their children to the park and simply sit. It was a luxury I couldn't even fathom.

I wanted to be the radiant young woman who I had seen in my spiritual encounter, a vision of myself surrounded by love and light. I hated the frazzled, stressed out woman I had become. I wanted to be the amazing woman who raised three handicapped children and juggled a household of seven successfully. I wanted to be courageous and inspiring, despite insurmountable odds. I wanted to do the impossible. And I did, but it wasn't courageous or inspiring. It was a struggle, and through it all, I felt like a failure. My work as a wife and mother was a disgrace, I believed, and it seared my soul.

All of these feelings—anger, resentment, fear—worried me. *What kind of a mother thinks this way? After all the sacred realizations I've had about my children, how can I fail them?* I couldn't find the answers, not here, not now, and the effort to move us out of state became more urgent.

March 25, 2001
Plans are still underway to move to Utah in July. All three girls are in one bedroom now. Quinn has his own room and Shale still sleeps with us in our room. We have entirely outgrown this house. It gets more crowded every day. I'll soon be 32 years old. My mother was that age when she died. It's more real than ever.

Life took on a surreal quality, as if everything was happening all around me, and I was merely an observer. Something was drawing me to Utah—something significant. I could feel it. I cared for the children every day, but my vision was fixed on someplace better. Out there, I would find relief from my suffering. Out there, I would find a new life. I felt like time was running out. This move was my last hope, and it was remarkable how everything fell into place so quickly. It seemed that what would have normally been impossible for our family occurred with remarkable swiftness.

Summer came, and so did dozens of family and friends to help us pack up. It was like a circus, juggling the children, the house, and the boxes. The only thing that kept me sane was the hope I felt in my heart for a better life far away. It was driving me, drawing me, urging me forward.

While packing up files one day, I happened to come upon my mother's death certificate. I pulled it out and examined it carefully. I had never read it before. It was yellowed and worn around the edges, and the letters were crinkled and faded. I ran my fingers over the delicate paper, remembering for a moment. DECEMBER 26, 1977. I scanned the page, and then my eyes froze on the line CAUSE OF DEATH. I did a double take, and read it over again to make sure. HEART FAILURE. Maybe it was customary to list cause of death as heart failure for cancer patients, but I couldn't shake the sadness that swept over me. I looked down at my mother's wedding ring on my left hand that I had been wearing for the last nine years. It suddenly seemed so frail.

* * * * * * *

Kyle travelled to Utah at the end of June to find us a rental house while I stayed home with our children and finished packing. Before he left, we discussed the necessary features the home would need—the number of bedrooms, bathrooms, a yard for the children to play in, and a layout that would accommodate our unusual requirements. After viewing several houses, he found one he liked and paid a deposit. We made all the financial arrangements from California, signing a lease for one year. I could hardly contain my excitement for the new house. At last, everything was set.

In July, we made the trek to Utah over a period of two days, sleeping only three hours in between. Driving the moving van ourselves slowed us considerably. What would have normally taken twelve hours ended up taking over eighteen hours. By the time we arrived in Salt Lake, we were exhausted. We turned into an old, shabby housing tract lined with homes built in the 1970s. As soon as we approached the house, my heart sank. It was a dive. There were broken windows, old stained carpet, and trash still lying around.

There had been a plumbing leak recently and the carpets were all pulled back. A small fan was propped up to blow it dry, filling the entire house with the musty smell of mold. The bedrooms were dingy and dark, and there was a freaky laundry room in the basement with a drain in the middle of the floor where, the neighbors later informed us, a rat had once lived. I was disgusted. This was my new home, and it was awful. Then I had a morbid thought: *There's nothing that Quinn can do to wreck this place*, and I actually heaved a sick little sigh of relief.

Immediately, the neighbors came out to help us move in. It was time to introduce these poor unsuspecting people to our unique family. I had hoped we wouldn't stand out as much here, but I already felt like a spectacle.

August was spent unpacking and getting our children situated. Everything was different here: the climate, the culture, and the schools. Integrating into our new lives would take time. The following month, on September 11, the twin towers in New York collapsed in a shocking and brutal terrorist attack. I put my children on the school bus that day and sent them out into a world that seemed suddenly unsafe. I felt so vulnerable in a community of strangers, miles away from dear friends and family and in the grasp of an already-radical life change. Phone lines were overloaded for hours, preventing me from reaching out for the support and comfort I so badly needed. News reports and horrifying live footage played continuously from our television throughout the following days, adding to the mounting anxiety in the air. Alarming commentary regarding potential risks to the upcoming 2002 Winter Olympics in Salt Lake City heightened the tension we all felt. Returning to normal life seemed impossible, at best.

In the fall, my dad retired and my parents made preparations for a service mission to the Midwestern states. They would be gone for eighteen months, enough time for us to get settled and build our custom home before they returned. My parents came to stay with us for a few days prior to leaving, and during that time we shared stories and reminisced. It was so comforting to have them there, strong and stalwart. The day they left, Jaede and I stood on the porch and watched as they drove away. When they disappeared around the corner, she and I held each other and cried. We both felt something of hopelessness in their absence. Though I was happy for their new adventure, I was terrified not to have my mom and dad close for support during this time.

My journal entries became substantially less frequent, sometimes months apart.

> *January 10, 2002*
> *Last week I felt so discouraged. I felt as if we would never get to build our*
> *house. But this morning Kyle and I prayed that this would all work out.*
> *Since then I have felt better. It has been a rather emotional three months.*

Our new life in Utah was not what I hoped it would be. I wanted a new start, an opportunity for happiness and peace. I believed there was a spiritual force drawing me here—I had felt it. But the house was depressing, and caring for the children grew more difficult each week. My life had gone from bad to worse. Still I tried to be positive.

We enrolled Quinn and Shale in a special school for children with disabilities. I felt good about the placement and was impressed with the facility. The staff members were attentive, and having my sons in the right program seemed promising. I affirmed to myself that we had made the right decision to move.

Every few months, I attended educational planning meetings to bring the school staff up to speed on my sons' needs. Kyle still traveled to California for work, leaving me alone with the children for weeks at a time. It was intimidating sitting at the head of the large conference table surrounded by professionals wanting to hear about Quinn and Shale. I hoped they wouldn't see the anguish on my face as I spoke of my sons' challenges. Sometimes it took all I had not to break down in tears during those meetings. I couldn't understand why after all these years, it still felt painful that my children were disabled.

While they were in school, I spent all day cleaning and fixing up our house to be fully functioning and Quinn-proof. We replaced the broken windows, had the air ducts professionally cleaned, and reorganized the kitchen. We put up a solid wood gate at its main entrance, as well as a half-wall to close off the other entrance, to prevent Quinn and Shale from getting in. They had broken in before and pillaged the entire refrigerator and pantry. Quinn had also figured out how to turn on the gas stove; the blue flame fascinated him. Keeping the kitchen inaccessible was paramount to our children's safety.

Next, I tackled the scary laundry-bathroom in the basement. I scrubbed and cleaned every corner of cobwebs and grime in that room and bought a rug to cover the rat drain. I installed new fixtures and dispatched several spiders. Lastly, I doused the room with industrial-strength air freshener. When it was done, I unveiled it to Jaede for personal validation, then locked it from the inside and closed the door. Bathrooms were also unsafe for Quinn and Shale.

Our doorknobs were all equipped with locks. Personal belongings were targeted for destruction by both Quinn and Shale. We also installed a double-sided dead bolt on the front door to prevent dangerous escapes. If I needed to open the door for anything, such as checking the mail or greeting a visitor, I had to use a key. Quinn and Shale were confined to the living room and hallways only. Unfortunately, so were the rest of us. This presented a problem for Psalm who was toilet training at the time. If I couldn't unlock the bathroom door soon enough for her, she would have an accident.

I had tried multiple times over the years to toilet train Quinn and Shale, but had no success. Their bladders were so active, they went through a wet diaper every hour. Between Quinn, Shale, and Psalm, I changed a diaper literally every thirty minutes. Our house smelled like human waste all the time. I tried all varieties of air fresheners and deodorizers, but nothing eliminated that smell. The grime, the gunk, the waste was more than skin deep. It was soul deep.

There were no pictures on our walls, no curtains, no lamps, no accessories of any kind. We had two shabby thrift-store sofas and a television that continuously played the same cartoon musicals we had been watching for the last ten years. I kept all of my pictures and valuables packed away. The house was bare, the walls were bare, and there was no color, no cheer, and no creative expression of any kind. I went into auto-pilot mode to cope with the oppression and protect myself from the pain.

Quinn discovered the thermostat in the hallway and frequently turned it up or down all the way. Ironically, he managed to turn up the heat in the summer, but turn it completely off in the winter. He also developed an obsession with the light switches, turning them off repeatedly throughout the day. He loved the darkness; so we, too, lived in darkness. Our home had become someplace ugly and depressing, despite my continuous efforts to make it cheerful.

All of the fulfilling things I had once done—the mentoring, the poetry, the acting—had disintegrated. It seemed the world outside my front door was just a side note, a mirage really, like some mythical legend in which I had once been a character. I ventured out occasionally to buy groceries or run errands or to put my children on the school bus, but otherwise I was housebound.

A large window which faced the street sprawled across our front room, and every day I watched neighbors come out of their houses and go to work, or walk by with their dog, or drive by in their cars. People came and went out there, but I was locked in my own house. I held the key, but it was made void by the limitations placed on me by those I loved. I was bound by my own obligation to them, held captive by the uncontrollable circumstances that I fought on a daily basis to control.

In the fall, leaves fell like opportunities blowing away in the wind, and in the winter the cold chill settled on me like a gripping stronghold. I had to stay. Day in and day out, I had to stay. So it was that we lived in a dark, bare, diaper-smelling house that was locked with a key from the inside. It was a prison.

And I was a prisoner.

CHAPTER TWENTY-ONE
Dying

In February, we bought an acre of land in a quiet suburb just south of Salt Lake City. The process had been a three-month fiasco of bogus brokers and lender screw-ups, but by June we had paid off the loan. When we applied for a construction loan to build our house, however, the mortgage lender expressed concern about our blueprints. Because the home had been designed specifically to accommodate our special needs, the bank saw it as a risky investment and denied us the loan. We felt discriminated against. There were many obstacles that kept popping up to prevent us from building our home. I would later learn this was an unseen force intervening in my life.

I began collecting antiques and furnishings, purchased through the mail, for our new house. I kept them safely in the garage, organizing them into groupings for each child's bedroom. I envisioned each room as a colorful and creative expression of their unique personalities. I fantasized about living in this beautiful dream home with a large playroom for Quinn and Shale, equipped with industrial carpet and a safe bathroom with modified bath fixtures. I visualized an area with all the things I loved—fresh flowers, bright colors, clean furniture, and pictures on the walls. Our new house would be filled with everything that was missing from my life now. It would be a sanctuary, a place of comfort and inspiration. Envisioning this haven of beauty helped me maintain my sanity.

My parents kept in touch during this time, calling every few weeks, and cautioned me to be sure I didn't overextend myself. Shortly after moving, we discovered, much to our dismay, that the state services we so badly needed were not readily available. Due to the extensive number of children in Utah, there was an enormously long waiting list for any help for my sons. Quinn was finally assigned a caseworker and a few meager respite hours, but Shale remained on the waiting list because he was not deemed "difficult enough" to warrant immediate aid. With the lack of services and Kyle's continuing work in California, the burden of caring for the children fell primarily on me.

My daily routine began with a wake-up call at 4 a.m. when Quinn banged on my bedroom door. This was his new method of getting my attention, and it was extremely effective. The loud pounding jolted me awake and I hit the ground running. I changed his diaper, dressed him, and gave him his first meal of the day. After this, he usually needed another diaper change. Then I put in a cartoon video and handed him his favorite toys, but he invariably pulled me to the kitchen for more food. About this time, Shale woke up, and I changed and dressed him, and gave him breakfast. I sat up with both of them, making sure they stayed out of trouble and didn't wake their sisters. I also cleaned up the vomit that was typical during mealtime.

Quinn had developed a new behavior of removing his clothes and grinding on the floor. He was eleven years old now and was approaching adolescence. Self-stimulation was his new obsession, and keeping him clothed was a wardrobe feat. I bought one-piece jumpsuits and put them on him backwards, pinning the zipper in place so he couldn't unzip it. When that didn't work, I put two jumpsuits on him at once. However, somehow "Houdini" managed to get out of these and I was cleaning up feces everywhere.

All of this happened before 6 a.m.

When the girls awoke, I let them into the kitchen to fend for themselves, Faith at seven years old and Psalm, a mere three-and-a-half. They were like orphans. This was the only life they had ever known. Jaede watched the children while I showered—a five-minute splash of water and a quick change. There was no time for makeup, hair styling, or any other self-care. I felt ugly, dirty, and frumpy all of the time. I had always taken pride in my appearance, but as I peered into the mirror, I no longer recognized the woman staring back. Her eyes were empty and cold, strangely reminiscent of the haunting eyes I had seen in my mother's scrapbook.

On school days, I hustled to make lunches for all of my children and get them ready on time. Jaede and Faith walked around the corner to the neighborhood elementary school. Then the bus came, and I sent my sons off for what seemed like a very short school day. During this time, I cleaned the morning's messes, did laundry, dishes, food preparation for that evening, an occasional errand, and took care of Psalm. I picked up Faith from kindergarten and Jaede walked home shortly after. Once Quinn and Shale returned, it was non-stop again. Weekends were the most grueling. Unless Kyle was home to help, I couldn't take my children anywhere.

Quinn reigned supreme in our home. He intimidated his sisters as leverage against me. He would stand by one of them, posturing as a warning to me that he would pull their hair or shove them if I didn't give him what he wanted. He knew my vulnerabilities, and his messages were loud and clear. Quinn had reduced Shale to a miserable bundle of nerves. He incessantly grabbed or yelled at him throughout the day as a way of expressing his frustration. Shale lived in constant fear of Quinn. We all did.

Perhaps the most terrifying and disturbing behavior Quinn developed was biting. He gnawed constantly on his wrists and fingers as his stress levels elevated. His hands were red, grossly scarred, and often bloody. He also bit others brutally, leaving us all with bite marks.

Mealtime was a unique adventure. We all ate meals in shifts. Jaede, Faith, and Psalm ate in the kitchen by themselves, while Kyle and I ate in the front room, feeding Quinn and Shale from our own plates. Quinn and Shale also grazed on snacks all day long.

At bedtime, Quinn put himself to bed when he was ready, but Shale required a lot of coaxing. Kyle or I had to sit with him for thirty minutes or more, patting his back softly until he fell asleep. After tucking in all of our children, I locked all of their doors from the inside so that Quinn couldn't disturb them during the night. I worried constantly about the hazards of doing this, but the alternative was pure chaos. Around ten or eleven o'clock at night, I stumbled into bed thoroughly spent.

I began living hour-to-hour, then minute-to-minute. I was way beyond survival mode by this time. I began crying frequently. I cried while vacuuming or changing diapers, while preparing meals or bathing my children. Sometimes I waited until I was alone in the car where no one would see. At night while everyone slept, I often went into the living room where I sat and cried in the darkness. I felt like I had been forsaken—by God, my husband, my children, even friends and family. My parents were engaged full-time in their new adventure and were unavailable to come to my aid. My little sister remained as distant and volatile as ever, and my two stepsisters had families of their own and were unaware of the magnitude of my predicament. I felt completely deserted, like no one in the world knew of my suffering. And, in fact, they didn't.

I was grateful for the days when Kyle was home to help. He still watched a lot of television and played computer games, but he also changed diapers and helped feed the children. I longed for more time alone with him. However, we needed professional childcare with special needs experience, an expensive and complicated task in an oversaturated community. Bedtime was our only opportunity to enjoy one another, but Kyle couldn't stay awake past nine o'clock. And I was too exhausted anyway.

Intimacy was rare. I couldn't shake the emptiness I felt from it. It had become my impersonal duty, a ritual of necessity, and it was disheartening and deeply unfulfilling for me. Our intimate life disintegrated under this environment. There was no tenderness or nurturing and rarely any kissing. He seldom even looked at me during the experience. I felt like I could've been anyone lying there. Afterwards, I often cried silently in that dark, dingy bedroom. I had become truly faceless.

My outer life and inner life spiraled downward rapidly. I was overworked and under-loved. I was utterly depleted, and I felt invisible to the outside world. The isolation was paralyzing. One time at church, a woman approached me and asked, "Are you the mother of the retarded children?" That's who I was to everyone. Even the ladies assigned to visit me asked only how Kyle and the children were doing, never how *I* was doing. Kyle had a life outside of our home, a creative outlet through his business, and recognition and praise from people who knew us. His work in California was thriving, and he had the ability to pursue his interests. But I had nothing, and I was a nobody. In a house full of people, I felt completely alone.

Record hot temperatures left our house sweltering that summer. Without air conditioning, we cooked like an oven. Early one morning while I was in the bathroom getting ready, Quinn reached over the kitchen gate and grabbed a three-pound bag of chocolate chips. He and Shale gorged themselves, spilling the entire bag all over the living room. There was melted chocolate everywhere—on the sofa, the walls, in the carpet, and my sons were covered from head to toe. It had been mere minutes that I had left them alone. I spent the next several hours cleaning it up.

One night that week, I woke up sweating. It felt as though there was a fire burning somewhere in the house, and I stumbled out to the hallway to check the bedrooms. There was no fire, but the heat was suffocating. I checked the thermostat: *ninety degrees*. Quinn had woken up sometime during the night and turned up the furnace all the way. I switched it off and started crying. Immediately, I went into the kitchen to cool my face with the tap water, but the water ran hot. I next tried the bathroom faucet, but it was scalding. I let the tap run for several minutes to try and flush out the hot water, but it never cooled. Frantically, I ran downstairs into the basement laundry-bathroom and turned on the tap there. Scorching hot. *What is happening?* Then I looked above my head and noticed the water pipes for the entire house positioned right beside the furnace that had been running at full capacity for hours. I returned to bed weeping and weary.

When Kyle came home from California the following week, I told him I needed to talk. Things had gotten out of control and I was miserable. I made a list of everything in my life that needed to change. The list was a full page-and-a-half of simple things such as self-spraying air freshener to reduce the constant smell of dirty diapers in our home, time to research my interests like acting classes and film programs, a date night once a week, and a family dinner every day with our daughters so we could enjoy one meal without vomit. In tears, I told him of my unhappiness, my overwhelming stress, and my lack of fulfillment. I pleaded with him to help me make changes. This was my last cry for help. Kyle sat patiently and listened. When I was finished, he agreed to help me.

We decided to start with a family meal once a day. The plan was for me to make a separate dinner for Quinn and Shale each night and feed them first. Then I would take them out of the kitchen and make dinner for the rest of us. Our table would be set with the nicest dishes and a pretty centerpiece, something to brighten the experience. The five of us—Kyle and I, along with our three girls—would sit down and enjoy a peaceful meal together. The process would entail a lot of work for me, but it would be worth it.

The first time we tried this, Quinn and Shale yelled at the kitchen gate in protest as we ate dinner. Even though they had just eaten, it angered them that we were eating without them. So Kyle brought Shale in to eat with us. Though Shale was more manageable than Quinn, he still gagged on his food and made a mess at the table. Jaede looked at me, disappointed. We had just wanted one normal experience as a family. The next time we attempted this, Quinn and Shale yelled at the gate even louder. Finally, Kyle picked up his plate and looked at me.

"You are so selfish," he said, then walked out of the kitchen to feed them.

I looked at Jaede with tears in my eyes. I realized then that nothing would change. Kyle did not see the urgency in our situation. He did not feel our pain. We were *all* suffering. And what hurt the most was that this was acceptable to him.

I was lost. I lay in bed at night visualizing myself getting into my car and driving away. I pictured my dingy house growing smaller in the distance, then finding a long, lonely highway where I could drive for miles and miles and never be found. I became despondent. I began crying myself to sleep every night.

We revisited the possibility of placing Quinn in another group home. Kyle knew that Quinn's needs exceeded my capacity to meet them, but he told me it was ultimately our responsibility to care for him. He was our son, after all. I worried constantly about my inability to offer my children anything more than the most basic survival. I couldn't teach or train them to become more self-sufficient in any way. It took every ounce of my life force just to manage their basic daily needs. Kyle talked about changing our sons' diapers when we were old and gray, romanticizing the idea that we were martyrs caring for our helpless sons till the day we died.

Divorce was not an option. I knew I couldn't care for my children alone long-term, and I knew no one would ever want me. Besides, my marriage was a commitment to be kept at all costs; I had been taught that my whole life. We were the amazing "success story." I couldn't let down my family, my parents, or those who still looked up to us. The comments continued about how heroic our family was. I felt enormous pressure to live up to that ideal. I also still felt the promise of two young, bright-eyed kids out to conquer the world, crazy in love, and with enough aspirations to last an eternity. That had been us at one time. It seemed like a million years ago.

I wanted to return to that night Kyle asked me to marry him. Had we only known the tumultuous journey that lay ahead, we might have held each other close for a little longer and savored the togetherness that would later become a terrible rarity in our marriage. Had we been able to see five years into the future, we might have chosen to map out a different course, to wait several years before having children and only have one or two. We might have gone into our marriage bracing ourselves for adversity, arming ourselves with the courage and strength that would later become so vital to our survival. But it was too late. We were just kids raising kids, striving for an elusive happiness that seemed always out of reach and struggling to make our way through an impossible situation.

I don't know the exact moment I began dying. It was so subtle, almost imperceptible. Excepting for the emptiness in my eyes, there were no physical signs or outward symptoms. I still woke up every morning, tended to my husband and children, and went to bed every night. But inside me, something was very different. I no longer saw the miracles around me or the joy in my children's innocence. I no longer saw the face of God in the sublime or the fragile. All of these things were now cloaked by my despair. I no longer felt at peace with the past, nor hope for the future, and I could no longer abide the present.

In my mind's eye, I stood on the edge of a towering cliff, peering out over a vast abyss of lost and broken dreams. In it lay my visions of happiness and a life of meaning, now scattered like dusty, dry rocks crumbled at the bottom. I could never be a good mother or give my children the kind of life they needed. It was too much for one person to do. I could never be content with the role Kyle expected of me. I could never be an actress who inspired people or made films that touched lives. My creative expression was like the sand under my feet—cold and lifeless. In all of these things I had failed miserably, defeated by the absolute immovability of our circumstance. I took a step closer and a few rocks rolled over the edge. Behind me the wind was howling, daring me to jump.

I could never again be the hopeful little girl with stars in her eyes who had the courage to dream and the vision to believe. In fact, I would never do anything that anyone would ever know about. The world would never know who I had been.

I shut my eyes and tried to feel something, but I felt nothing. There was no life in me. There was no *me*. I was like the walking dead in the land of the living. I needed to find a way out—a way that would keep my marriage intact, protect my children, and leave me with dignity. I searched for any possible option, but I saw nothing. I looked for hope, but found none. Only one choice remained. I held my breath . . . and stepped off the ledge.

I was praying for death.

CHAPTER TWENTY-TWO
The Unseen Beside Me

For the first year we lived in Utah, Kyle and I took turns going to church with our daughters each week, while the other one stayed home with Quinn and Shale. But when Kyle began teaching a Sunday School class, I stayed home and cared for our sons every week. After a year, our church finally made arrangements to accommodate our sons' special needs, enabling us both to attend our Sunday meetings. A team of volunteers was trained, and I was eagerly looking forward to refilling my spiritual well.

As I sat in class the first Sunday of this new arrangement, I heard Quinn yelling in the next room. My stomach tensed, and I looked around to see if anyone else had heard it. A few minutes passed, and he grew angrier. I tried to ignore the muffled tantrum on the other side of the wall and instead listen to the teacher's peaceful message, but my palms were sweaty and my heart pounded. *How can I sit here while Quinn has a meltdown with total strangers?* As soon as class ended, I jumped up and rushed out of the room to rescue them.

When I arrived, they were surprisingly calm despite Quinn's and Shale's frustration. The teachers were very kind, and the sacrifice they were making on my behalf deeply moved me. One of the teachers was a man named Dan. He and Kyle had worked together on a few construction projects that year, and we began spending time with him and his wife. The social experience gave me the first lift I'd had in years and was a welcomed retreat.

* * * * * *

Thanksgiving came, and we took a trip to visit Kyle's relatives. Though Quinn's behaviors had kept us from attending most extended family gatherings, we decided to give it a try again. It turned out to be a nightmare. Quinn was furious, lashing out at us the moment we arrived. Kyle took him for a walk to try to calm him down, but when they returned, Quinn was covered in blood. He had bitten large chunks of skin off both arms and was in a gruesome adrenaline frenzy. I was mortified. Kyle's family helped with our other children while he and I stayed awake with Quinn all night.

The next day was our Thanksgiving feast, but I was emotionally done. I quickly packed our things and made preparations to leave immediately following the meal. Afterward, we stood outside the house—Kyle gripping Quinn, me holding Shale, and our three girls huddled in-between—while everyone snapped photos. I felt like we were on display. I told Kyle I was never going back again.

At home, we continued spending time with our friend, Dan, and his wife. We met together a few times at the end of November to play games or watch a video after the children were in bed. Normally I would have been exhausted at the end of the day, but I found myself looking forward to those nights.

December arrived, and we put up an ornament-free Christmas tree in our living room, strapped to the wall so Quinn and Shale couldn't tip it over. Our house was the usual disaster, and it didn't feel at all like the holidays. Quinn and Shale had a Christmas program at school one night, but Kyle and Jaede decided to attend a Karate class instead. So I piled my four youngest children in the car and took them to the program myself.

At the school, my sons' teachers could see that I was overwhelmed, but I put on a smile like I always did. Afterwards they offered to help me out to my van, but I declined; I wanted to get out of there as quickly as possible. A frozen darkness had settled in the air, and snow began falling as I hurried through the parking lot. Quinn was agitated before even getting into the van.

I put him and Shale in the back seat at opposite ends and strapped them in. I buckled Faith into the bench seat in front of them, and I put Psalm in her car seat on the front passenger seat. Then I drove away from the school and headed onto the icy freeway in what would become the most perilous ride of my life.

A few minutes into the drive, Quinn's agitation intensified into yelling. This triggered Shale, who began crying. Suddenly, Quinn erupted into the fiercest psychotic episode I had ever seen. The harness still bound him to the seat, but he had managed to get out of his seatbelt and was lunging at Shale wildly, screaming and tearing at his face. Shale cried out in terror, but there was nothing he could do.

"Quinn, stop!" I screamed, "Quinn, *please stop!*"

I fought to control the van on the slippery highway, rushing to get home as fast as possible. Quinn continued attacking Shale and himself, tearing at his own wrists, blood everywhere. My heart was pounding. Then he lunged forward for a lock of Faith's hair.

"Maaaaaama!" she shrieked.

"Faith, undo your seatbelt and get up here, *now!*" I shouted.

She quickly fumbled out of her seatbelt and huddled down onto the floor next to Psalm's seat. They were both trembling.

Quinn was in a rage, lashing out violently at Shale—only because he happened to be the one sitting closest. Shale screamed in agony as Quinn tore at his face and head and arms. I looked in my rearview mirror and gasped at Shale's bloody face. He cried out again, wailing at the top of his lungs. I was paralyzed. My helpless son was being assaulted by his own brother, and I was powerless to stop it. If I pulled over now, there would be nowhere to contain Quinn while I protected the other children. I had to get home.

"God, please make him stop!" I demanded, tears pouring down my face. "Where are you? Why won't you help us?"

Blood oozed from Quinn's self-inflicted bites on his wrists and arms as he panted and shrieked viciously. Helpless, I watched the horrific scene from my rearview mirror. Shale's wailing amplified even more, and Faith and Psalm were shaking and crying in the front seat.

Time stood still. Cars passed by on the freeway, but we were someplace else—in a different world. It was surreal. My whole body shook. I had never felt so terrified.

Then I saw it: the underpass.

A vision flashed before my eyes of the van driving full-speed into the concrete wall, instantly killing all of us. I tightened my grip around the steering wheel and pushed the gas pedal to the floor. I wanted our suffering to be over. I wanted us to be out of our misery. As far as I could see, the misery was going to last for years to come. I kept my eye on that underpass. It was coming closer. I needed to make a choice. I knew it would be a terrible thing to do, but keeping us in this miserable situation was terrible, too. Only it was indefinite; there was no end in sight. I could turn my steering wheel now and end it in an instant.

I took a deep breath, and the underpass whizzed by.

Something, somehow, kept me driving.

I drove the rest of the way home in a daze. When I pulled in front of our house, I noticed Kyle and Jaede had not yet returned. Instinctively, I grabbed Shale first and carried him inside, taking him straight to his room. He shook uncontrollably the whole way. In the light of his bedroom, I saw the full extent of his injuries: bite marks, scratches, bruises, and blood covered his entire upper body and face. He was still trying to catch his breath. I carefully laid him down on his bed and locked his door so he would be safe. Then I hurried back to the van.

Quinn was still strapped to his harness, and Faith and Psalm sat wide-eyed and trembling in the front seat. I quickly swept both girls into my arms and carried them inside to their bedroom.

"Don't come out. It will be okay," I assured them.

They huddled together, their faces drenched with tears. Then I locked their door and went back for Quinn.

I approached the van cautiously. Quinn was panting and heaving, and he had a crazed look in his eyes. My hands trembled so badly I could hardly undo his harness. I muscled him out of his seat and walked him carefully into the house. He tried to bite me several times, but I held him tight. We went straight to his room where I laid him on his bed. After a moment, he relaxed and settled into the covers.

Later that night, Kyle and Jaede returned home as if nothing had happened. I told them about Quinn's episode, and Kyle became alarmed when he saw Shale's bloody face.

How could you have let this happen? He seemed to say.

I never told Kyle about the underpass.

PART FIVE

A Redeeming Love

CHAPTER TWENTY-THREE
Rebirth

During this time of unspeakable despair, my friendship with Dan and his wife became a rare gift and a true miracle for me. After the children went to bed each night, the four of us met to play games, watch a video, or enjoy dinner. The despair I had felt for so long slowly dissolved as I relearned how to relax and have fun again. My mind gradually detached from the stresses of my daily life, and I put my attention to the unexpected awakening that was taking place within me.

I began pulling clothes and shoes out of my closet that I hadn't worn in years. I styled my hair and wore makeup again. I put on jewelry and perfume and painted my nails. I even danced in my kitchen. As I made the time for these important but long-forgotten remnants of self-care, my spirit revived, my heart gladdened, and my body energized. Even the color returned to my face. One night upon finishing my makeup, I stood back and took a long look at myself in the mirror. I recognized the girl staring back at me. Her eyes I knew—those bright, hopeful eyes. They almost had stars in them again.

Thoughts of Dan flowed into my mind throughout the day as I went about my daily routine. His broad smile and hearty laugh cheered me. His energetic presence and vibrant face inspired me, and I found myself looking forward to seeing him each night. I loved the way his eyes lit up when he looked at me. He seemed attentive to my needs, and I loved how I felt when I was near him—like I *mattered*. He listened intently to my ideas and opinions, offering me the respect I had been lacking. I was intrigued by his sense of confidence. I, myself, had once been that confident. Though the challenges with my children continued, they somehow didn't bother me as much. I was the first one on the phone to plan our next get-together and the first one at the door each evening as they arrived. I became stalwart, driven by a powerful impulse.

Christmas came and our family opened gifts, ate Christmas dinner, and spent the day together. But my thoughts were someplace else. I was a new person, vibrantly alive. Just weeks before, I had sought death, groping aimlessly in the dark for a way out. I had prayed for an escape from my hopelessness, stood at the brink of the abyss, and had come back. Something now gave me a reason to live, and I didn't fight it. In fact, I accepted it fully and allowed every part of myself to surrender to it. I was in love with Dan. Like a rare oasis in the savage wilderness of my life, I had found a curative spring—life-giving waters that healed and resuscitated me, infusing me with new life-force. Its hold over me was utter and absolute.

Dan reached out to me in subtle ways during this time. His awareness of my plight heightened, and he stepped up to help me at home and in the community. He volunteered to work with Quinn and Shale more at church, as well. His compassion moved me, and I felt compelled to approach him. One day, while my children were in school, and Psalm was napping, I called him. Kyle had gone to work, and I was alone in my bedroom.

As I dialed Dan's number, my heart began pounding. Though I had never done anything like this before, I was fiercely driven to continue.

The phone rang several times, and then his strong yet gentle voice answered.

"Hi, Dan," I said. I hesitated, suddenly shy.

"Hi, LeeAnn."

I could feel the blood rushing to my face. "Do you have a minute? I want to ask you something."

"Sure," he said in his usual cheerful manner, completely unaware of the bomb I was about to drop.

Long pause.

"Are you attracted to me?" I blurted out awkwardly.

He let out a sudden nervous laugh. My face reddened even deeper. Then he paused for what seemed an eternity.

"Yes," he replied, "I am."

A powerful tingle ran up my spine.

"I'm attracted to you, too," I confessed.

My heart raced wildly, and adrenaline shot through my body.

"Would you consider holding me?" I couldn't stop now.

He paused again, and I wondered if maybe I had taken it too far. Maybe he would reject my request.

"Yes," he said. "I would hold you."

This moment shifted my course. There would be no turning back. It was every bit as scary as standing at the edge of the cliff, only this felt death-*defying*. Rather than stepping off the ledge and plummeting, I would leap off and soar. My heart had been dead, my experience had been dead, and my world had been dead. But Dan was life. And I wanted to live again.

In January, we began a love affair. While Kyle was at work, and my children were in school, I arranged for a babysitter for Psalm, so Dan and I could spend time together. Being in his arms during those brief encounters was unspeakably exhilarating. I was so caught up in the experience I hardly ate or slept for two months. My entire being was charged with electrifying hope. All the years of disappointment and sorrow suddenly evaporated in a beautiful and passionate experience with Dan. The loneliness and heartache instantly vanished, and the burdens I had carried alone the last several years lifted all at once. I celebrated unsparingly the newness and vigor of this love being awakened inside me. It was magnificent, and I relished every second, every breath with him. All thoughts of death fled—I was fully alive now. That pivotal, transformative cherishing I had yearned for was being given— freely and unrestrained—through the timeless gift of Dan's love.

I learned that I was not sexually dysfunctional, as Kyle and I had presumed our entire fourteen-year marriage. I was sensual, powerful, and dazzling. I learned that I was still full of life, and that it wasn't too late for me. In the embrace of someone who was fully present, I learned that I could be happy—truly, deeply happy. And I realized there was untold hope yet for my future. Dan expressed his desire to take on my children, handicaps and all, and to give us a new life. He opened my eyes to all that I had accomplished and all that I was doing for my children.

"LeeAnn," he said to me one day, "you are a *great* mother."

January 30, 2003

A new year is here! We're still working on getting a loan for our new house. Do you think it will ever be built? Only time will tell.

The only journal entry I wrote during this period was brief and vague. I couldn't bring myself to write about what was happening between Dan and me; it was too personal. And I had never written about crying myself to sleep at night, or praying for death, or the underpass. Somehow, putting it all on paper had seemed too painful, too real, and I wanted to protect myself from it. All of January and February I remained disconnected, mentally and emotionally, from everything that was happening at home, including our plans for the future. I went through the motions of my daily tasks, but my heart was eons away. Our affair lasted two months, from New Years Eve to the end of February.

As suddenly and as powerfully as I had ascended, my world came crashing down more suddenly and more powerfully the morning I told Kyle.

"I have to tell you something you're not going to like," I began.

We were lying in bed one morning, and Quinn had just begun pounding on our door.

"What?" Kyle asked, the beginnings of concern evident in his voice.

I knew I had to be direct, that softening the information would not serve this moment. The words formed in my mind, and somehow I found the strength to say them.

"Dan and I are having an affair."

Kyle jumped up and whirled around to face me.

"How much of an affair?" he demanded, in a sudden panic.

"Completely."

He was devastated. The last time I had heard a man cry like that was my father's anguished sobbing following my mother's death. Telling him and watching his reaction was one of the very worst experiences of my life. Kyle wanted me to stay, but I knew I could never be happy with him after my relationship with Dan. I knew I could never go back to having no life of my own. I had reached the end.

Kyle pleaded with me, telling me that if I had given him an ultimatum, he would have listened. If he had known that I would leave him when things didn't change, he said, he would have helped me. If I had only given him the choice between me and the children, he told me, he would have chosen me.

But it was too little, too late.

I dressed the children for school and waited until the bus came. Then I got in my van and drove away as I had envisioned myself doing so many times. I didn't know where I was going; I simply had to leave. I ended up in a nearby hotel. Within a few hours, Kyle found where I was staying and called my room.

"Come back," he pleaded, his voice quiet and low.

The weight of what I had done and the impending condemnation from those who would soon find out fell over me with crushing force. I had never so much as looked at another man our entire marriage. Raised and cultivated in a standard of stellar moral code, I was now suffocating under the massive breach of its violation. I knew what the "right" thing to do was, or at least what everyone would tell me was the right thing—to return home to Kyle. But still I did not want to go back. It would be all too easy for others to urge me to stay in my dismal marriage, to encourage me to return to a home where I was not cared for, but they didn't have to live it. I was profoundly distraught. Kyle urged me to make a choice right then and there. The pressure was so great, I felt I would implode.

"I need time," I told him. "I'm not ready to make a decision yet."

"What will you do?" he persisted.

"I don't know."

I hung up the phone. That night I couldn't eat. I couldn't sleep. I couldn't even feel my own skin. I knew I was in trouble. My weight had dropped dangerously low. I had lost twenty pounds during the affair and was now a mere one hundred pounds. A new feeling pervaded my body—the feeling that it was too late to save myself. Only a few months before, I had prayed earnestly for death. Now, I pled for my life.

The next morning, I went back to Kyle.

CHAPTER TWENTY-FOUR
Haunting Choice

As soon as I saw Kyle, I knew I had made a mistake. He immediately put me on what felt like house arrest. I couldn't make phone calls, receive visitors, or even leave the house. This was done, he said, to protect me from stress. But I knew it was because he didn't trust me. Our home became my prison again. I felt vulnerable, broken, and entirely powerless.

Kyle had informed Dan's wife of the affair, and I knew that she and Dan were in the midst of their own turmoil. My heart ached for their family, for his wife and for his two children. I never wanted to hurt her, but now I felt the certainty of her pain that I had helped to inflict. I was struggling with feelings I felt no one in the world could understand. Then one day as I was reading through my old poetry, a voice from my past spoke.

"These things are happening to you because you're so much like me."

It was my mother, Carol. *But what did she mean?*

* * * * * *

The following days after my return, Kyle and I began communicating openly, perhaps for the first time in our marriage. The dark clouds that hovered menacingly over our lives began to part, shedding understanding on our hearts and clearing away misperceptions that had built up over a decade and a half. He confided in me that, despite what he had told me when we were dating, he had always wanted a large family. Suddenly, his carelessness with the condom all those years made sense, and my heart was torn between the bitterness I felt by what he had done to me and compassion for the painful irony of his actions.

"All I ever wanted was to be a dad," he confessed.

He admitted that if we had placed Quinn in a group home permanently, he would have resented me for it forever. His honesty was brutal, but starkly eye-opening. He then told me that he, too, had fallen in love with someone else during our marriage.

Kyle was in rare form. He listened attentively while I recounted for him my feelings through our years together. We began to see that we had not communicated honestly in our marriage. Except for the few moments of tearful pleadings for help, I had kept my sorrow to myself. I had neglected to express to him my disappointments, my anguish in caring for the children, my lack of fulfillment in our sexual relationship, and my fears for the future. He, too, had not been forthright in his expectations of me as a wife and mother. We realized how vital honest communication is to a successful marriage, and how ours had suffered dramatically from the lack of it. The enormous toll on our relationship by our disabled children was also now fully evident, having driven us forward in a devastatingly intense workload from which there had been no rest. My life had become an endless routine of diapers, feedings, violent behaviors, and stress. A breakdown was inevitable.

With our family in crisis mode, we now had to make some hard choices regarding our sons. We had been told that services were not available for Quinn or Shale, that the waiting list for any permanent help for them was enormously long, and that they would most likely never receive it. Our sons required a level of care we could not offer them, no matter the magnitude of our efforts. We needed to garner the help of the state, to make it clear that we could no longer care for Quinn and Shale alone. We knew there was only one way to do this. We also knew that in the process, we might possibly be arrested and lose everything. Time was crucial and we had to act immediately.

There comes a moment, a painfully clarifying moment, when we see that in order to best serve those we love, we must let them go. In this moment, we find ourselves looking through a lens of firm and unforgiving reality, a dark place where choices return to haunt us and where light seems to glimmer only from a distance. In order to go toward that light and relinquish further suffering, we must embrace the loss that accompanies it. We must choose to let go of our ideas cast in paralyzing stone and become something different, bendable to the cruel but necessary requirements of life's deepest trenches. For Kyle and me, this moment came in early March 2003.

Quinn and Shale clamored at our front door, anxious to venture outside. Kyle carefully took them by the hand and walked them to the van, strapping them in securely to their car seats. I sat alone in my bedroom, in anguish for the task I knew was in motion and still confined to the house. Kyle drove several miles to the temporary care facility for children with disabilities and pulled in front of the building, unsure of the sequence of events that would follow. Quinn and Shale gave their usual protests from the backseat, unaware of the pivotal moment at hand. Kyle unbuckled their seatbelts and led them inside where disabled children and professional staff milled about. Kyle held tight to our boys' hands as people filed in and out. After a moment, he released his grip. Then he turned around and walked out, leaving our precious sons to fend for themselves.

Moments later, Kyle arrived to a home that was all too quiet, all too still. He walked straight to our bedroom and without saying a word, sat down next to me on the bed. We had let them go, Quinn with his potentially violent temper and Shale with his desperate vulnerabilities. We loved our sons more than words could say and to have them out there, defenseless and alone, was unspeakably heartwrenching. I reached for Kyle's hand, and we both began crying.

We had abandoned our sons.

Chapter Twenty-Five
Found Again

Immediately, phone calls began coming in. The police were summoned and our sons were taken from place to place for days. Our phone rang off the hook, and practically every agency in the state stepped in. It was hell. A thick fog enveloped me.

Kyle's family came to our aid and was there to help with our daughters during this time. Jaede, in particular, was very distraught about the massive changes being thrust upon her. She was not only concerned for her brothers' welfare, but she was also highly anxious about her parents' relationship. Faith and Psalm were too young to understand the implications of what was happening, but having our household turned upside down was very upsetting to them. Literally overnight, everything in our lives had changed. My parents were four states away in the process of making arrangements to come help, but Kyle's family lent the support and sanity we needed to get through those first few weeks.

Our caseworker was called in to help us determine the next step for Quinn and Shale. As we shared with her the details of what had transpired, she cried with us, stepping up to advocate for us like never before. It was determined that our sons would enter professional placement. We met with the state agency to take us through the process. At a certain point during our conversation, the term "foster care" was mentioned. I became alarmed. *Will my sons be living in a foster home?* I had heard of foster children being adopted by their foster parents. *Will they still be mine?* This meeting only solidified my previous feelings that I was a failure as a mother. Afterwards, I felt a new level of loss. I cried for days.

* * * * * * *

In the middle of March, Kyle and I separated. I moved into a small cottage, and Kyle rented a one-bedroom apartment literally next door to me. I was a wreck. I was so distraught I couldn't eat or sleep. I missed Dan terribly, but I couldn't bear to tell Kyle that our marriage was over. He and our three girls were crammed into his tiny one-bedroom apartment to give me the space I needed to figure things out. I felt like my life was hanging by a thread.

In his rare generosity during those agonizing days, Kyle helped me set up my new house. It was strange to be with him in a home we wouldn't be sharing. We hardly spoke, but we went about arranging the rooms with all of my beautiful things that had been packed away for years. We dressed flowers for the table and hung pictures on the walls. We draped lace curtains over the windows and set out my vintage poetry books. We laid out pretty linens and strung dried flowers from the valances. I realized how important these things were for my morale. I had lived for too many years without them, but now beauty could surround me. I needed this added boost to get through the vulnerable months that followed.

His last night with me in my little cottage, Kyle and I made love more passionately than we ever had before. Afterwards, we wept openly, mourning our failed marriage. Kyle was my first true love, and the tragedy of it all was palpable. Our lives together had been like an epic movie filled with brave heroes cast into the fire, overcoming the most daunting of obstacles and emerging victorious. Only our ending was all wrong. There should have been victory for all the promise of our future and the light in our eyes when we started out on this journey together.

But there was no victory now. We held each other close. This would be our last night together.

* * * * * * *

In the coming days, Kyle came over and made me breakfast each morning. He became surprisingly concerned during this time. Though he flipped between thoughtful care and angry frustration, he somehow managed to help me get back on my feet a little.

One morning he remarked, "I think I'm being helped through this," and I knew what he meant. He was being strengthened by an unseen source. I wanted to tell him that I still saw greatness in him, that it wasn't until I gave up on me that I actually gave up on us. I wanted to tell him that I never stopped loving him. But the words would remain unspoken.

For two weeks, Kyle helped me regain my strength, and during that time, he wrote me letters—poignant, beautiful letters penned by a man who was no longer blind. In them, he spoke eloquently of my talents and my beauty, offering me inspiring messages of hope. They were like parting words from a love long lost, and they filled the air with a wistful melancholy.

My heart became a receptacle for every emotion possible. For years, I had been numb to the events around me. Feelings were reserved for those who had the time and energy to respond to their environment. I had been on automatic pilot for so long, in a mode of desperate survival, that my emotional receptors had become anesthetized. But now I was feeling loss, frustration, relief, and hope in a painful yet bittersweet kaleidoscope of emotion.

I knew in my heart it was time to reconnect with heaven. I also knew that I would have to face accountability. The devastation of my actions was now in full view. Friends, family, and even strangers were made aware of and became affected by the affair. I had been the cause of great pain to many people, shattering their trust and respect. The disappointment I felt for ruining my "perfect marriage" was crushing. Our family had been a source of inspiration to many people, but now it seemed I had destroyed that.

As I knelt by my bedside to offer up my first supplication in three months, the air was dense and daunting, and my heart heavy with the ten-ton weight of self-condemnation. I closed my eyes and bowed my head, and I felt a lump form in my throat.

"Dear Father in Heaven," I nervously began, "please forgive me."

I expected to feel the searing wrath of a disapproving God or the suffocating guilt of my terrible deeds. But the instant I opened my mouth, something unexpected happened: a feeling of compassion and empathy washed over me. The sensation of complete understanding came forcefully into my heart. I opened my eyes and looked around, bewildered. *How can this be happening?* A sense of wonder filled me, and I experienced His presence in a flawless and beautiful embrace of unconditional love.

I had been taught about unconditional love in Sunday School growing up, but this was different. This was *real*. This made the hair on my arms stand and my heart pound in my chest. It was so expansive and freeing, any previous notions I held about God being a condemning diety were suddenly void. All at once I understood the uselessness in judging ourselves and others. How useless it suddenly seemed to suppose we know what is in another's heart. I realized the presumption I had displayed in judging others over the years. How foolish and self-righteous I had been. In the past, I would have harshly criticized someone in my position. But here, in this moment, such judgment was rendered meaningless, and I felt liberated from the trappings of self-condemnation and guilt. I was not being judged or condemned now. I was being loved. I was simply and perfectly loved. There was no searing wrath, only peace, and matchless love.

The heavy denseness of my sorrow lifted, drifting into the air above me and dissipating in the light of my bedroom. I sat facing heavenward and allowed this feeling of warmth and comfort to surround me. And I began to heal.

I came to know the nature of God in that moment. He wasn't some mysterious being who sat high in the heavens peering down at me, and He wasn't a remote deity whose impossible expectations I had failed to meet. He was very personal and intimate, and was so close I could practically feel

His breath on the back of my neck. Like a gentle and loving father, He was there with me in that room, watching over me in the deepest sense. He knew the reasons behind my every action, even better than I did. There was no condition to His love; it was freely given. There was no prerequisite to His respect; he adored me just the way I was. My worth was great in His sight, regardless of my mistakes. And there was no fiery punishment waiting to be inflicted. He understood my pain, my despair, and my cries for help. He had heard all those prayers—every single one of them. I had never actually been alone, not for one fraction of a second. His face had been laid bare in all of the most majestic moments of my life, and in the fathomless depths of my suffering as well. He was fully present in every breath I had ever taken. And He took that broken, longing little girl in His arms and gave her His forgiveness.

Though friends, church members, loved ones, and even strangers all shunned me, I knew that God still believed in me. And, with that knowledge, I could find my way again.

A few days later, on March 28—my thirty-fourth birthday—Dan came back into my life, and Kyle took our girls to be with his family. It was official. Our marriage was over.

Being with Dan, I slowly revived. He had done something for me that no one else could. He brought me back from the dead.

One night, while cuddling, I casually punched him in the arm. It started as a joke, but I soon found myself kicking and hitting him hard, going after him with everything I had. Dan blocked my punches, but I lunged at him wildly, arms flailing in a fury. *Where is this anger coming from?* I didn't know, but Dan seemed to understand, and he let me go at him. Sobbing fiercely now, I swung and kicked at him with every last ounce of muscle I had left in me.

"Why did you take so long to find me?!" I finally shouted. The words stunned me. I was actually mad at him for not rescuing me sooner.

Dan took hold of my arms and gently wrestled me to the ground. Then taking my face in his hands, he said, "LeeAnn, *I love you.*"

A surge of energy shot through my body, electrifying me and piercing me to the soul. I *knew* it was true. I released into his arms, breathing out the burden of a thousand battles.

That night, with Dan's help, I wrote page after page of painful memories from my past. The words flowed freely, quickly, and abundantly as I wrote of my resentments for the unthinkable things I had been subjected to. I wrote of the horrific experiences I had endured. I needed to get it all on paper. I had been to hell and back, and I wanted the universe to know. For hours I wrote in detail of each hurt, each mistake, and each regret. Pain welled up inside me as I wrote about my assumed failures as a mother. I mourned that I had not done more, or done better, to help care for my children. I wrote of my fierce love for them and of my anguish in giving them up. And then I apologized. All down one side of the page and onto the next, my pen scribbled furiously: *I'm sorry, I'm sorry, I'm sorry, I'm sorry, I'm sorry, I'm sorry, I'm sorry.*

I'm sorry.

I set down my pen and dropped my head. The pain was now in ink, my past on paper. In my hand I held the experiences that represented every fire I had passed through. It was now four in the morning. Dan and I took the stack of papers out to the driveway, dozens of pages worth, and laid them on his truck bed. One by one we burned them, watching the ash float away with the wind. I stood there, tears falling from my cheeks, feeling the power of that moment.

Afterwards, we held each other in the cold, dark, smoky air. Neither of us spoke a word. Words were ash.

And I was now through the fire.

CHAPTER TWENTY-SIX
A New Beginning

In April, my parents took a temporary leave from their service mission to come be with me. Though they were upset at first with what I had done, they truly sought to understand. I began to see a counselor to help me work through the pain and loss, and my parents decided to attend a session with me in order to gain greater insight into what was happening. At the end of the session, however, my parents had more questions than answers. *How will they ever support me again?* I wondered. I slept fitfully that night, not knowing if we would ever reach an understanding.

The next morning, my parents showed up unexpectedly at my door. Something had changed—dramatically. They entered cheerfully and sat down. I immediately felt their warmth and compassion, and the stress I had experienced the night before instantly dissolved.

"Last night, when we were praying to understand better the reasons for what you did," my dad began, "to try and get a handle on all of this, something interesting happened."

I was curious, *What possibly could have changed their minds overnight?*

"We really wanted to help you," he continued, "but we didn't know how. Then as we pondered your situation, we were given these specific words: 'LeeAnn was dead and now she lives. Kyle was blind and now he sees.'"

My dad went on to explain how their minds had been opened, how they were given to comprehend my suffering and the reasons for my actions. They described how a clear understanding came into their hearts that these changes were necessary, and that all of us—me and Kyle, Dan and his wife, and even

Quinn and Shale—would ultimately be better off. This understanding was a revelation, and relief flooded the room. My parents then took me in their arms and held me close. Everything was going to be okay.

They wanted to meet Dan, so we arranged a visit at my home the following day. When Dan arrived, my parents were taken aback by his broad smile and cheerful countenance. For an hour, Dan told them of his own life's experiences and his hopes for the future. His wife had become pregnant while they were dating in high school. Three days after they told their parents of the pregnancy, a marriage was performed. At eighteen years old, Dan had a wife and new baby to support. He was working two jobs and going to school full time. His childhood had ended abruptly. He had always felt he didn't really choose his marriage, but that it was chosen for him. He, too, had experienced a kind of reviving through our relationship.

When we finished talking, my parents actually gave us their blessing. I was speechless. They offered their love and encouragement for me to move forward in my new life with Dan. It was unreal how everything was unfolding.

Our last day together before my parents returned to their mission post, we sat in my little kitchen and ate pizza together. I told them of burning the pages in the early morning hours with Dan. I told them of my anger, my regrets, and my apologies. I broke down and cried, and let all the pain spill out again. The floodgates of my past opened, and all the hurt and loss of my life came rushing back. For an hour, they cried with me. The pain was so thick, it was almost tangible. When it was over, my entire body was limp and aching. My parents helped me to my bed where my father left me with a prayer. In it, he referred to me by my maiden name. This was significant to me. I was a new person, and I was starting a new life.

* * * * * * *

Quinn and Shale were placed in two separate homes with professional parents. Their extreme incompatibilities and high-impact needs required each of them to be placed individually. The program was a long-term foster care placement where they would remain until they were adults. And they could never be adopted. Kyle and I could have as much involvement as we chose and would be expected to meet with the state court twice a year to give an update on their care. Each boy was assigned agencies to lend assistance and resources, providing the professional parents with everything they would need to successfully care for our sons. The parents that were selected were loving and compassionate, highly trained to manage children with disabilities. Both families spent adequate time with Quinn and Shale prior to their placement to ensure a strong match. Kyle and I familiarized ourselves with these individuals, visiting the homes where Quinn and Shale would be living and giving our full support for the arrangement. I knew that I, too, was being helped through this experience by an unseen source. Giving up my sons was unbearable, and though it was strange to see them with a family other than ours, I took comfort in knowing they would finally have the proper care I was never able to give them.

In the coming months, Kyle and I filed for divorce. And Dan proposed to me. Our wedding was scheduled for June 7 and my divorce was not final until June 5. We had sent out invitations and planned a beautiful wedding. It was a major miracle that I was divorced in time.

The clerk at the courthouse who handled my divorce papers worked very hard for me. She went out of her way to push through my divorce much faster than was typical. I'm not sure why she was so driven to help me; I was a complete stranger to her. But she called me daily to give me updates, and she finally took the forms directly to the judge herself to get them signed. The papers were finalized with just two days to spare.

Our beautiful wedding ceremony was held in a stately historic mansion. Vibrant yellow flowers—the color symbolizing hope for Dan and me both, a gorgeous tiered cake surrounded by real rose petals, and stirring music created an unforgettable beginning to our marriage. It was truly enchanting. But what amazed me the most was that people actually came.

December 5, 2003

One of the most humbling and remarkable blessings during this experience has been the immediate understanding and support of my family. Both my immediate and extended family responded with support for my decision as I transitioned to a new life with Dan. I think they knew before I did that my life could not continue the way it was. I miss my sons, but I know they are better off. There are major repercussions to what I did, but it has been a necessary change in my life. I have a new direction now. My story has a new ending. A heavy price was paid for this opportunity and I intend to make the very most of it. God has given me a second chance.

How grateful I am.

CHAPTER TWENTY-SEVEN
Little Girl Realized

After a weeklong honeymoon in Fiji among beautiful white sands and palm trees, Dan and I returned to Salt Lake where I signed with a local talent agent to begin modeling. I also threw myself into acting and enrolled in a new class. All kinds of opportunities became available to me, and the limitations that had previously held me down no longer bound me. However, having lived through continuously intense situations for twelve years since Quinn's birth, my first response to any conflict was a stress response. I felt frantic oftentimes and became easily panicked. Lingering posttraumatic stress disorder triggered bouts of weeping whenever I was in close proximity to the dismal house where my life fell apart. I still cried myself to sleep at times, struggling to make sense of the opposing emotions that wrestled in my heart—guilt for the major changes Quinn and Shale were undergoing, while feeling elated with my new life. It felt strange, even wrong, to be operating under the notion that I was a priority. I had felt so neglected and unloved by Kyle for so long. But Dan took me fully into his heart, embracing me with a kind of love that was all-encompassing and truly transformative.

That fall, Dan and I made a trip to California to visit the house where I had lived as a little girl. We also visited my former elementary school as well as the school where my mother had been teaching when she died—all places which represented the deepest part of my childhood. Giant butterflies fluttered in my stomach and long-forgotten memories came rolling back. It seemed there was an alternate world out there like shadows of a past life, and stepping back into the scenery of that life made me an observer, walking among the familiar ghosts and hollow voices that inhabited it. A little girl had once lived and dreamed there, surrounded by love and hope and shooting stars.

We made a special trip to visit my mother's grave, something I had wanted to do for many years. The cemetery was enormous, and people were gathered, huddled under tents and in chapels to mourn the loss of their own beloved ones. The morning was overcast, but eerie and beautiful, not unlike the day of my mother's funeral. As Dan and I walked along the grassy pathway, I noticed flowers planted near the gravesites. It saddened me that I had never planted flowers here. When we reached my mother's grave marker, it glistened with morning dew. It felt emotionally powerful standing above it, and prickly chills ran up and down my spine. It read: CAROL M. TAYLOR, OUR LOVED ONE.

I knelt onto the cool, wet grass and placed a bouquet of roses onto her grave and said, "I love you."

The words went out from my lips and disappeared into the morning mist. My entire body tingled as I knelt on that hallowed ground, and I felt things about my mother I hadn't felt since she was alive. The feelings were instinctual and unexpectedly strong. I sensed her somehow, as if I was eight years old again, even down to the smell of her gardenia perfume. We were getting ready together, and I could see her standing in her bathroom, curling my hair. I heard the sound of my laughter, a silly little girl with a heart full of hope. I thought if I returned to that old house, I might find her medicine bottles and lotions still lining the shelves, maybe covered in a little dust. She would be playing *Moonlight Sonata* on her clarinet, and Beethoven would be watching on.

I stood up and looked out over the rolling hills of the cemetery dotted with grave markers accumulated over decades. She had been here for almost twenty-six years herself, buried under layers of dirt and memories. It was truly tragic.

Chapter Twenty-Eight
Hope Rising

Even though my life had changed for the better, many unanswered questions still loomed in my mind. I struggled with the fact that I had given my sons to professional care. *Have I done the right thing? Why couldn't I help them more? Did I fail them?* These questions haunted me, causing many sleepless nights that first year. I felt guilty and inadequate and I hoped my sons could one day forgive me. As hard as it had been caring for them—as harrowing and all-consuming as it was—giving them up was infinitely harder, and I wondered if I would ever find peace.

Then on the night of June 20, 2004, the answers came. I had retired to bed late but hadn't fallen asleep yet. A profound stillness settled on me, and I became unusually serene. Then a familiar voice spoke through the darkness to my heart.

"You've been thinking about me a lot lately."

I knew that voice, its gentle wonder, and the powerful love behind it. It belonged to my mother. I immediately sensed her spirit hovering over my bed, and I became instantly energized. Then words began flowing rapidly into my understanding.

"In your spirit existence," she began, *"you had already learned to master happiness. You came to this world as a strong and vibrant shining star, LeeAnn, and your life has been filled with pain to teach you to overcome the negative. The instant we learn what God is trying to teach us, our particular trial is lifted. In your life, instead of looking back and seeing pain, you can look and see the positive."*

She then showed me specifically how to do this.

"In your early childhood, you learned happiness; you mastered it. When I died, you learned self-reliance. During the following years of puberty without a mother, you learned survivalism. When your dad married your stepmother, and you lived with her and your two new stepsisters, you learned to adapt. When you married Kyle, you learned faith; you were meant to be together. When your children were born and you raised them, you learned all the facets of love. You learned to love the unlovable. When you and Kyle separated, and you suffered tremendous pain and fear, you learned management. When you moved forward with your life, you learned resilience."

These key words were emphasized with exactness. I now saw how the challenges of my life had turned to benefit me, and by the lessons learned, I had grown exponentially.

"LeeAnn, seek out positive affirmations to remind yourself of your capability, the inspirations you've received, and the spiritual experiences associated with them. Fill your life with positive thoughts, words, feelings, actions, and energy. Put yourself in a place of success. Success, both spiritual and temporal, is based on the principles of positive and negative energies. Success is an actual place," she revealed, *"a sphere where positive energy flows forward like a stream. It is a stream of positive energy. When an individual is successful in any arena, whether in their career, or financially, or in athletics, they discover the 'place of success.' They are 'riding in the stream.' They can be people of all walks of life, religious or not. It doesn't matter because the principles of positive and negative energies are eternal laws and are applicable to us all."*

Into my mind's eye came a vision of a large planet-like sphere where tubes of energy flowed rapidly forward like streams of light in a current. They wove in and around one another in a stunning display of light. I saw individuals riding in these streams, coming in and out at different times during their lives. They would retain this light throughout their lifetime, I understood, if they stayed in the momentum of the flow.

"*Cling to positive energy, LeeAnn. Sift out the negative, like a sieve. Glean the positive from everything; discard the negative. In all things in life, take the positive. Success will be attracted to your positive energy and will connect. As for the rest of your life,*" she warned, "*the amount of negative energy and trials depends on you. If you remember to always cling to the positive, you can avoid trials.*"

"Please help me remember how to do this, Mom," I asked.

"*At this time, you are on a positive plane,*" she noted.

My thoughts turned to Quinn and Shale and the private sorrow that still haunted me.

"*It is not for them to forgive you.*"

I was startled. "How could that be possible?"

"*Did you intentionally hurt them?*"

"No," I replied.

"*Did you really ever hate them?*"

"No."

"*Did you do as much for them as you possibly could?*"

"Yes."

"*Then they have no need to forgive you,*" she stated. "*You, in fact, showed the ultimate love for them when you gave them up. Keeping them would have been selfish. Giving them up was the best thing for them, LeeAnn. Because it was so painful for you, it was the true test of love. And when you see them in heaven, it will be as if you've known them forever—completely familiar.*"

I thought of my sons' impaired cognition and how it served as a cloak, concealing their true identity from me. I yearned to know them more fully.

"*Quinn and Shale were best friends in their former spirit life,*" she continued. "*They desired to come into mortality together, in the same family line. They were highly evolved beings and had accomplished much of their spiritual progress before being born. They chose their afflictions—their specific disabilities. You, too, chose to bear those afflictions in caring for them, knowing that you would need those survival skills for the important work you would do later in your life. Your sons are emissaries, sent to mortality to teach others compassion.*"

The power of that statement hit me forcefully. I had been witness to my sons' divine qualities numerous times. I had been given a glimpse of their angelic natures. Now I was being shown that they were pristine vessels in malformed bodies and impaired intellects here to touch humanity in a most unique way, evolving us all to higher spirituality. A humbling and newfound love infused my soul for Quinn and Shale, and they became even more amazing in my eyes.

"Your work with your sons is not finished, LeeAnn," she assured me. *"You will yet have the opportunity to fulfill a sacred work together. This will be revealed to you at a later date."*

She went on to explain to me about Kyle and his challenges, *"Understand that Kyle's selfishness was never malicious, but it was selfish nonetheless. He could never have allowed you to be who you wanted and needed to be."*

I beheld a vision of the front room in our little condo. It was so clear, every detail, even down to the dust particles in the sunlight that streamed through the window. And it opened up to me as though I stood right in the midst of it:

The television was playing a cartoon video. In one corner of the room, Quinn was spinning a ball and growling. He was three years old, and his disability was evident. In the middle of the floor, Shale was lying on his stomach, fixated on an object, with his whole body stiffened. He was just a baby. Though his disability was also evident, I had not yet detected it. The room was cluttered with toys scattered everywhere. Little Jaede came in and out of the room, exploring imaginatively, so carefree and innocent. I stood watching everything that was happening, fully aware of everyone. I had "spiritual feelers" out to them, like spikes of energy or vibrations on an aura. And I was tuned in both mentally and spiritually to their needs. As a mother, I absorbed everything in my environment and was greatly affected by it. My emotional investment was tremendous. That's why it hurt so much.

Then Kyle walked through the door, just returning from work. He was wearing his yellow polo shirt and jeans. He came in and put down his keys on the table, but I saw how he wasn't really aware of what was happening or how we were all feeling. He wasn't present. It's as if he wasn't truly *there*. He was only aware of himself and his own needs. But I loved him, and I tuned into his needs, becoming aware of him in every sense. He was aloof and was therefore protected from the pain and suffering of our situation. He carried a fragment of the emotional burden, but I carried all the rest by myself. I saw that I was never meant to carry the burden alone; it was too much for one person to bear. I also saw that because he only carried a fragment, he therefore received only a fragment of the blessings and growth from those opportunities.

I was shown that we are sent hundreds of opportunities every day to learn about love, some large and some small. We can either choose to capture those opportunities, or we can let them go. The choice is ours. If we choose to capture them, we are blessed by our personal growth and the outcome of those opportunities. If we choose to let them go, there is neither punishment nor condemnation. That is not who God is. Our forfeited growth and blessings are punishment enough.

I saw that even though Kyle no longer had the opportunity to learn about love from me and our children in that setting, he still had the opportunity in a modified version. He could choose to capture it, or he could let it go. I realized there was no need for me to forgive Kyle for how he treated our family, for his indifference and disregard. His actions were neither right nor wrong. They were neither good nor bad. They simply *were*. Understanding healed my heart, and peace replaced the sadness that still gripped me.

She continued speaking firmly, but with infinite love, *"LeeAnn, realize that information comes to us as we are prepared to receive it."*

She then revealed to me something that would shift my entire life:

"I chose death as a way out."

Her words shocked me.

"I, like you, wasn't allowed or enabled to be myself—my strong, bright, ambitious self. I was a very social and bubbly young woman, and I cared deeply about what people thought of me. After marrying, I had to pull back my personality. I felt stifled and hopeless. I felt smothered. I looked for an escape, but

there was none. I saw that I would never be happy in my marriage, but I couldn't disappoint others. I was very obligated, and therefore, I didn't consider divorce an option. I couldn't see any other way out of my oppression, LeeAnn. So I chose death. I willed myself to get cancer."

This information hurt me deeply, and I felt the sorrow of her needless death as never before. But there was more for me to know.

"By so doing, I had to save the life of another in order to reconcile my mistake. For when a life is forfeited, a life must be saved. LeeAnn, I orchestrated the meeting of you and Dan as an act of intervention. You would have literally died had you stayed in your previous situation with Kyle and your sons. You would have taken your own life in a matter of months."

The chilling truth of that pronouncement and its untold devastation sobered me.

"I intervened to save your life, LeeAnn. In a way, Dan saved us both."

My mother's words sank deeply into my heart. I felt the monumental weight of those words and all of the implications associated with them. I sensed the connection with my mother anew—an ironically tragic, yet triumphant connection.

"In addition to your life being saved, the generational pattern was stopped," she taught. *"You unknowingly perpetuated a generational pattern of suffering that I had started. You repeated my pain and error in succumbing to the burdens that beset you. You, too, stayed trapped in your hopeless situation, choosing to suffer and die rather than make the necessary changes to remove yourself and find happiness."*

The irony of our parallel struggles, independent of one another and separated by decades and death, was stark. At the same time, a powerful resonance sprung into my heart, filling all the gaps left by her absence for the last twenty-six years.

She and I were so alike, in all of our most human frailties. She, too, grappled with the paradox within her: the peace of her warm baths contrasted with the inner despair that overshadowed her. The stifling oppression she felt despite her independent free spirit. It all seemed so strange, yet so familiar. Everything made sense now—the dispirited photos of her in the scrapbook, the death certificate stating heart failure, her change of heart after the cancer. I felt the tragedy of my mother's young life cut short, the trauma of her disease, and her slow decline to death. I felt the vibrancy of her spirit gradually weaken and her life's plans disintegrate. Like me, she was a bright, vivacious girl who held onto life until it seemed too much to bear. Her artistic expression and love were evidences that she was reaching out, trying to salvage her happiness. Like me, she hid her pain from everyone—her parents, her children, her husband. It wasn't until she was actually dying that she realized how precious life was. It wasn't until her life was being taken away that she realized she wasn't ready to relinquish it. But by that time it was too late. None of us could reach out and rescue her from death like she had just rescued me. None of us could throw her a rope and pull her to safety. It was sobering.

Her intervention was not just the help of a loving mother for her daughter, it was a necessary act needed to reconcile her death. There was so much at stake. Until my life was saved, until I had broken the generational pattern that threatened to follow my daughters if not stopped, my mother was not free to move on in her own spiritual journey.

The truth she spoke was powerful. I wanted to know more. I wanted to know *everything*.

"Why did you choose Dan?" I asked.

"Dan is a very special young man," she replied. *"He has all the right qualities. Realize your connection to Dan is spiritual—it was from the beginning. During the affair, your intimate relations were positive because of what they did for you. They made you feel alive again—happy, bright, and hopeful. Sex is very misunderstood. It is, in fact, spiritual. Even the touching we do engenders that vibrant sensation that our spirits feel when we are in heaven. The connection between you and Dan is very powerful."* She then added cautiously, *"Put positive energy toward your relationship with him. There will be times when it will be needed."*

I could sense my mother's joy in sharing these understandings. She then explained why she and I were able to communicate so freely.

"In mortality, we sometimes become so weighed down by stress, worries, or worldly distractions that we can't see clearly. The veil separating us from heaven becomes more like a curtain—thick and dark. Also, the veil between us and our 'True Environment' becomes thick and dark, disabling us from seeing mortality in its true form. There are two veils. And when we are disbelieving, we do not allow heavenly spirits to contact us."

My mind was opened and my heart weightless; for this reason, the veil was thin. I also found in our communication that my mother wanted me to figure out many of the answers myself. I finally understood that I had made the right choice to give Quinn and Shale to professional care. This knowledge wiped away all the sorrow and anguish I had been carrying the past year. It was profoundly healing. I knew now that my sons loved me and that my actions did not warrant their forgiveness. I had done my very best; I had given everything I could to them. And it *was* enough. Though I understood the pain associated with my past, I now had the perspective to see the benefits I had gained from those experiences. I understood that my new life with Dan was appointed for me and that we were capable of doing great things together. I understood that my mother's suffering and hopelessness had become my own, and through a generational pattern I, too, was facing imminent death. I learned that there are patterns within families that continue to perpetuate needless suffering until someone stops them. I also learned that it is entirely possible to bring disease and death upon ourselves by our very *thoughts*.

The stain of Christmas tainted by my mother's death was also given new light. Even though I had always perceived it as a tragedy that she died the day after Christmas, I was now shown that it was meant as a gift. She was barely able to get out of bed Christmas morning, and it was that very night that she slipped into a coma. But we were given that last holiday to spend together. I could feel joy and peace in celebrating that sacred holiday. I could let go of the sorrow with every song and every symbol of that day. I could reaffirm my belief in miracles, and be ever thankful for a mother's parting gift.

"Please stay close to me, Mom," I asked.

"I am never very far, LeeAnn," she said, *"I have been with you all along. It was I who awakened your spirituality as a young girl and who gave you understanding of the love God has for you. I gave Shale and Quinn mothering at those times you were not able to. It was I who carried you through the refiner's fire when you could not go another day, and it was I who showed you the value of your suffering. I came to offer myself as a support while you carried your burdens alone, and then I lifted them off your shoulders to enable you to move on. I showered you with my joy when you received the news of Psalm's test results, and I held your hand when you cried yourself to sleep. I came many times as the angel in the corner of the room, and I was the unseen hand that kept you from driving into the underpass. I gave your parents the inspired impressions that you were dead but now live, that Kyle was blind but now sees. I am the orchestrator of your sons' new placement and the architect of your new life with Dan. I was there with you at every turn and in every moment, my little porcelain doll. And I will be there still. I love you. I cherish you. And as you see, my daughter, I have never left you."*

These words rested powerfully on me, filling me with wonder. I allowed myself to feel them penetratingly. One after another, my mother had been there at every impasse in my life. At every touch point interceding, there to catch my every fall and hold me up by the redemptive power of her love.

I envisioned my mother preparing to continue on in her spiritual progression, a brighter and more brilliant being, free to move forward and upward now that she had saved my life and been redeemed. A timeless angel encased in light, she was moving on to a holier sphere, far beyond her earthly trials and suffering. I sensed her profound joy and excitement for her new journey ahead.

It was now two in the morning, and I was winding down. We had communicated for three hours. There was so much to think about, but there would be time for that tomorrow. The serene warmth of my mother's love enveloped me as I drifted into sleep.

As a young girl, my mother often took me to a park near our home where she pushed me on a swing. As I swung higher and higher, the wind blowing against my face, it seemed the earth was far below me and I could touch the sky with my feet. She loved to see that look in my eyes. Now as I lay drifting off into a kind of peaceful slumber, I seemed to touch the sky again, rising higher and higher and higher. The earth seemed far beneath, a distant sphere of moments and memories now healed.

My mother's spirit lingered like a warm embrace, filling the air around me, watching me, holding me, as I finally, deeply, fell asleep . . .

"You are a shining star whose time has come."

AFTERWORD

Since that night in June of 2004, I have experienced a rare closeness with my mother, affirming to me that a mother's work does not end at death. Indeed, there is nobility in motherhood and its implications are eternal. Guiding these precious children is a work that follows us beyond the grave. When I was struggling with what I perceived to be my "role" as a wife and mother, I had not yet gained a realization of the immense impact or the long-term effects a woman could bring about for her husband or her children. Now, I serve as a wife and mother who counts every detail as a contribution to the timeless welfare of her family. Womanhood is a lasting—even infinite—step toward higher evolution. This is my ultimate "role"—to be *love*, anywhere and everywhere I am. And to give all my energy and hope to the continuance of that love.

My mother's intercession on my behalf was a true indication of her love for me—that redeeming and higher form of devotion that reaches beyond this life into the eternities of our existence. When we feel divine intervention in our lives, we assume it is from God. But my mother taught me that it is often our departed loved ones who are stewards over us. They are willing to do whatever it takes to help us progress. Our spiritual growth is the most important thing to them. My mother has continued to be with me, guiding me with pure wisdom and teaching me sacred precepts pertaining to my life's work.

Shortly after our divine encounter that night, my mother joined me on Psalm's first day of kindergarten to share with me what would be a very unique experience. I walked Psalm to her new class and met her teacher. As we stood in the doorway and talked, I casually scanned the classroom. Inside, children were reading and playing and talking with one another. There were no adaptive chairs or classroom aids, no communication charts or diapers. Instead, bright alphabet cards lined the wall and colorful books filled the shelves. These children would be learning math and reading and history, and Psalm would be one of them. I savored the moment.

Afterwards, I walked slowly out to the parking lot just as a handicap bus was unloading a group of disabled students in front of the school. As the children came off the bus one by one, some in wheelchairs and some in special harnesses like the ones my sons wore, the teachers lovingly greeted each child. Like a scene from a movie, time seemed to stop. The vision of these afflicted children moved me, touching a part of me that was still very much alive. I slowed my steps and felt the wind brush across my face.

Then I heard my mother say to me, *"You don't have to do that anymore."*

Tears filled my eyes. That portion of my life was over. And it was bittersweet.

I vowed I would never forget how hard it had been for us. I promised myself I would never take for granted the things I could do now, like take my children to the park and just sit, eat a meal without vomit, hang pictures, sleep through the night, and put up a Christmas tree that actually has ornaments on it. I determined to be ever grateful for my new life but to never forget my former one. And I vowed to hold tight to the unspeakable gratitude that filled me.

My life continues unfolding gracefully. I have a remarkable bond with my father and stepmother today. They gather me into their accepting embrace and make me a cherished daughter. All I could have ever wanted as a child, I have been given as a woman by their loving and gifted hearts.

Kyle remarried one year after our divorce. My heart feels sorrow for the devastation I caused him and many other people by leaving our marriage in the way that I did. I know now, however, that I would have never left by any other means save death. And that would have been irrevocably tragic. I realize that my new life has come at a great price, and I treasure it with all of my heart. I am creating something truly magnificent with it. I feel both profound gratitude and wistful remorse for the monumental blessing of my deliverance.

Dan's former wife has also remarried and moved on. I will never know her struggle or the devastation I caused in her life. Nothing I do can ever take that back. I only hope that she finds greater happiness and peace than she has ever known. I have found great comfort in my mother's words regarding this woman, that *"ultimately she will be better off."*

Jaede is a woman now, a luminous and invincible star in my galaxy. For years, she felt like a half-child-half-adult living in a world of tattered beings. But today she is a compassionate, open-minded, and remarkably happy individual who accepts all people and celebrates life in everything she does. She is truly an inspiration. But I want to say to Jaede the child, *I feel your pain and I am mindful of you, darling daughter. I long to give to you violin lessons and build a playhouse for you. Yes, little girl, I was paying attention. I was listening. I love you so much.*

Jaede has since shared with me her own perspective regarding those dark years: "Mom, I felt like a river tree with roots that never touched the ground, always flowing continuously downstream in the current. I connected myself to the trees everywhere we moved. I loved the trees. When I climbed up and sat in them, my heart felt like it was traveling free to places my body couldn't go. I even see myself that way now—like that mythical river tree, with millions of intricate roots, traveling free and wild in the current, but never quite touching the ground."

Jaede is not just a survivor, she is a victor.

Quinn and Shale both live in professional homes, each with the support and services they need. They are thriving in their new lives. They have been with the same professional parents since the beginning. The two women who are mothering my sons are amazing, and their selfless love and devotion for Quinn and Shale have truly humbled me. It is difficult, however, to know that these caregivers wake up during the night with my sons, that they deal with their behaviors and needs every day. I understand the sacrifice better than anyone. Together, we are co-mothering in a way that is unique and quite beautiful. I visit with them regularly and enjoy my sons so much more, without resentment or fear. In fact, my heart leaps in anticipation of seeing them. For years, my mother was orchestrating a way for Quinn and Shale to have the help they needed. From beyond the grave, she prepared the way. I can now advocate for Quinn and Shale in ways I never could before. This is my gift to them.

Though I no longer guilt myself for giving up my sons, I want them to have relief from their challenges, from rocking against the wall and growling until their necks bulge. I want them to have friends and to fall in love, to hold still while I hug them, and to understand when I tell them I love them. I want them to have something for *them*. But I've realized they're not here for them. They're here for us. They're here to humble us, to open our eyes, to strip away our selfish pride and presumption, and to show us what is real. They're here because *we* are the ones with the special needs. Yes, Quinn and Shale are indeed angels, and I am truly privileged to be their mother. We have since begun our sacred work together that my mother promised me would be revealed, and I am learning just how magnificent my sons really are. This is their gift to me.

Faith is an angel in her own right and still has that delicate quality that engenders my sense of protection and nurturance. She can read and write and even has a charming sense of humor. Faith has been fortunate to be only moderately affected by Fragile X syndrome. The night I explained to her for the first time about her disability, she was twelve years old and unaware of how her limitations would affect her life.

"I'm not like Quinn and Shale, right, Mom? I just have a little Fragile X," she assured me.

After I explained the disorder to her in detail, she became unusually serious, "Will I have Fragile X forever, Mom?"

I paused for a moment, feeling my heart well up inside me. "No, Faith. One day you will leave this world and return to heaven as a bright angel, and you will no longer know limitations."

Raising a child with a disability is a beautiful experience, an opportunity to know the highest we are capable of and to transcend the lowest. It is an experience worth celebrating, even its darkest moments. For without these, we would never know the joy.

Psalm is still my miracle baby. She is so happy and light-hearted, a stark contrast to the life her siblings have known. Hers is a curious position: she no longer remembers the trauma of our former situation. That previous life is a distant shadow for her, mostly forgotten. I take her with me when I visit Quinn and Shale, but I don't push her to understand more than she is ready to.

Perhaps vicariously, Jaede, Carol, and I can experience through Faith and Psalm the childlike wonderment we may have been partially forfeited. Life has a way of coming full-circle. I'm now giving my daughters the kind of life I always wanted to give them. I listen to their ideas and foster their imaginations. I teach them to believe in themselves and to have dreams. I hold them close to my heart, making sure they're so very loved. By this, we recapture a moment from the past when a different mother helped her daughter feel the same way.

Though I choose to look forward on the new dawn of my horizon, I will always remember little girls with daydreams, violin lessons, and river trees. I will remember angels in the corner of the room, wistful love letters, and burning pages at 4 a.m. I will remember warm baths and blooming gardenias, and *Moonlight Sonata* on the clarinet. Even our most humble moments can be the cause of indescribable joy.

My new marriage to Dan is like the peace-giving waters that quenched all the consuming fires of my life. I do not doubt that I would have died had Dan not "found" me in time. He not only brought me back to life, he brought my life back to me. He reclaimed my childhood, my womanhood, and my hope for the future. He restored *all* of me. I love him deeply, and I am grateful every moment for his love for me. I am truly a cherished woman. We have a unique distinction in our union—a very unusual love story made possible by a very unusual intervention. Yet who knows the mysterious ways of God? And how could such controversy be divine? Because the life of just one individual is of divine worth in the heavens.

Along the way there were glimmers of hope extending out to me from many sources, but I did not reach out and capture that hope. Instead, I chose to wear a strong face and stay in my darkness. I now ask myself, *How long until we are honest with each other? How long until we realize that when I hurt, you hurt, and when we heal, the world heals?*

Before the affair, I was not only the blaring embodiment of loss, I was also a symbol of the harm that can occur when a person is denied love for so long. After the affair, I was condemned, shunned, and despised by many. Through the harrowing process that followed, I became refined—gleaned as it were—from the final remnants of my purification. The Gibraltar of my life had been reduced to gravel and I was now empowered to rebuild a monument of hope in its place. I learned to let go of judgment and the harmful effects of self-condemnation. I learned to love myself, and, by so doing, I learned to forgive.

I found that it is often through the greatest loss where we find the greatest gain. For years, I did the impossible with my children, fighting with every last thread of my will, yet I never quite sensed the courage of it all. I passed through the refiner's fire of my daily life and emerged perfected, but I couldn't see this until long after.

I am not a failure. I did not fail. I did not fail. I did not fail.

Those words are just an echo now, floating away like ashes of paper burnt on a cold, dark morning.

I had once believed that having disabled children prevented the work I felt driven to do in my life, but I have since discovered that it was in the lowest, darkest trials with them where my life's highest vision was born. It came to be, out of the darkness. And out of the darkness, came the Light. The cosmic co-existence of these two opposing forces creates a bewildering dichotomy that seeks to dismantle our naïve paradigms, as it bends and flexes its way through humanity like an unyielding thread. It is born in all of us—the Light—and we must find our strength by transcending the darkness. This is, and has been, the luminous charge that surges me forward—compelling me to light the way for others. I am now an author, award-winning filmmaker, and spiritual mentor for those who hope to transcend and triumph.

In all of my most impossible obstacles, through every defining second of my life, I had never known what limitless light was held within the human heart until I revealed that light within my own. Now I take these lessons— the radiant, ineffable treasures—and I share them with my fellowman that they, too, may see the Light in us all.

APPENDIX

Illuminations: Messages of Light from Beyond

The following teachings are from my mother's spirit, given in the sacred generosity of her love. I share them with you here that you may also receive of her light and be one with us.

Who Am I?

- We are spirit.
- We are divine beings, of divine heritage, and endowed with divine qualities.
- We are all of noble birthright.
- We are all gods in embryo.
- We are all made of light.
- We are eternal. We have always existed and will always exist.
- We are limitless.
- We are beings of infinite love, though we may not have "awakened" to it yet.
- We are agents unto ourselves, free to choose, and never bound by predestination or fate.
- We are capable of ultimate happiness and pure joy.
- We are perfection unrealized. Perfection is not flawlessness; it is *holiness.*
- We lived before this life and have existed for eons. We chose to come into a mortal life, take on a physical body, and fill the measure of our

creation by manifesting to the world our unique talents, gifts, and abilities. The world needs *us*. They need what only *we* can give them.

- All the tools necessary to navigate this mortal journey successfully already exist within us; they simply need to be "realized." Guides from beyond the veil can help us do this. So can enlightened people.

The Veil

- The term "veil" is used to denote a thin, transparent separation.
- There are two Veils.

The first is a *Veil of Forgetfulness* between us and the spirit world, drawn over us to conceal our former spirit identity from us. This is done so that we may experience the human condition without a remembrance of our former sacred home, for the purpose of enabling us to live completely in the moment and within the parameters of earth life; for example, being subject to time and space. This forgetfulness also enables us to endure the spiritual darkness that is often encountered in this world without the remembrance of a more perfect sphere. Were we to fully recall our former heavenly home, it would be nearly impossible to endure the challenges of earth life. We would be in constant conflict and wanting to return "home." However, there are little "remembrances" of our former spirit home, which will come to us throughout our lifetime. They will not reveal fully that heavenly sphere, but will give us the courage and strength to endure our trials here. They will serve as a beacon of light. Some of these remembrances will come from angels or departed loved ones and may be in the form of feelings of inspiration or enlightenment, which have a vague familiarity. Some of these remembrances may be a sense of belonging to a higher world, a distant home far away, or being a stranger here in this transitory state. Some may come from our own evolving to a higher level of consciousness—and from truth-seeking. When these remembrances occur, rejoice, for it is a sign that we are doing what we came here to do and drawing closer to our divine destiny.

The second veil is a *Veil of Truth* between us and our True Environment, drawn over us by our own stress, worries, and temporal distractions. This veil can become heavy and dark and can conceal from our view the true nature of our situation. This veil can also distort our perceptions, thereby cloaking our highest potential and disallowing us to resolve whatever particular problem we may be facing. This veil is only as heavy as we allow it to be by our distractions, our addictions, and our attachments to things such as money, materialism, and that which has no life. There will be glimmers of our True Environment that will shine through occasionally, and things will appear clear and simple. Our vision will shift and we will see things as they truly are. Remember the way things look and feel in this moment—calm, clear, and at peace. This is the true way of things.

- The transparency of both veils will fluctuate throughout our life, depending on the level of spirituality to which we attain and then maintain. The thinner the *Veil of Truth* becomes, the more conducive our environment will be to receiving divine guidance in our life and the more peaceful we will be. Chaos is always a barrier to this guidance. The thinner the *Veil of Forgetfulness* becomes, the closer our spirit guides will be to us. In fact, they are standing by at all times ready to help us. However, they are bound by our freedom and cannot violate it. We always have ultimate choice.

Piercing the Veil

- We are all spirit. Our departed loved ones still live. They exist in a spirit world. No one ever actually dies.
- It is possible, and indeed appointed for us, to communicate with

divine spirits and departed loved ones in order that we may exact the highest success in our earthly journey with their help. This requires us to accept that we are all collaborators on a path to ascension, and when we tap into a holy realm of light, our spirit will intuitively act in synchronicity with a divine guide. We will be led by their light and receive of the messages they have for us. This is called "piercing the veil" or "transcending the veil," and it is holy.

- In order to communicate with divine spirits, we must first attain a level of stillness in our lives. The more still we are, the more we will hear. Methods of attaining stillness include exercising gratitude, performing service for others, sincere prayer, quiet meditation, reading books of enlightenment, listening to stirring music, or watching inspirational films which depict individuals in a meaningful way. These practices evoke a sense of fullness where our spirits can expand and illuminate, creating a highly receptive state through which beings of light can communicate more freely.

- Retreating to a quiet place, in an hour of stillness, in order to prepare ourselves for divine communication is key. We must first designate a "sacred space"—a place of solitude, silence, and beauty that will be accessible to us on a continual basis. A separate room associated with peace and love, a secluded area outdoors in the midst of natural beauty, a quiet corner of our home conducive to positive thoughts and feelings; these are all possible places. Once a sacred space is designated, it will be sanctified by our intention to use it for this purpose. Spirit and light will be present in this space. We must then approach this space during hours of profound stillness, such as early morning before the sun arises. As the dawn emerges, a pervasive reverence hovers in the air. It is in this state where we will find divinity waiting.

- We must approach divine communication with humility and absolute belief. We must approach with absolute trust. Belief and trust are paramount. Unbelief, fear, and doubt are barriers to divine communication.

~ When possible, we must stand in honorable places. We must avoid places where irreverence or demeaning activity is common, such as bars or foul movies. Remember, we are preparing ourselves for higher things.

~ In order to receive inspiration for a specific challenge or need, we must be in the energy of that need. For example, if we seek to understand a relationship, we must be in contact with that person or deeply pondering our relationship with them. If we seek to receive inspiration about our career, we must be working, studying, and pondering continually about that career. It must be forefront in our heart. We must put intuitive energy to it before inspiration can come. Only then will our minds and hearts be prepared to receive.

~ We must submit ourselves to a place that exists one step beyond prayer and meditation. It is a listening space where we listen with our heart and not our ears. It is a gap where pure consciousness streams to and from our spirit. It is the dawn of divine intelligence.

~ When divine spirit speaks, the communication is clear and flows freely into our consciousness. It is never cluttered. It does not originate in our minds; rather it flows into our minds from a higher source. The communication is often spoken with words we would not use, or they are used in a way we would not typically use them. It is most often a still and subtle voice that is perceived and not audibly heard.

~ Sometimes, the inspiration may come as just a feeling or an understanding, and we may feel a sensation rather than thoughts or ideas. The impressions we've received will not soon leave, but will linger longer than a typical conversation. They may return to our mind often.

- Sometimes the impressions will be so subtle, we may be tempted to dismiss them. But we must trust them and their source. We must pay attention. We can immediately write them down and ponder them. If we choose to dismiss them, they may return less frequently.

- Listening, we will feel calm and open. *Illuminated.* We will never feel confused or fearful when a divine spirit is speaking to us. However, fear may lend a false interpretation to the experience. Given an inspiration, we may become afraid and thus associate that source with negative feelings. Rather than revealing the source of the impression in this case, fear would be an indicator of our own weakness and doubt. And when we doubt, the spirit will often withdraw.

- Divine inspirations will always lead us to positive action. They will never be harmful to anyone.

- After the inspiration has come, we will feel lighter, clearer, and our worries will be subdued. The eyes of our understanding will be opened and our sense of awareness will be heightened. The choices we are called upon to make will seem clearer and will be based on the principles shown us through spirit, not based on outside circumstances or emotions.

- The more we listen to and act from inspiration, the more we will receive. We are developing the ability to be a pure conduit for divine intelligence. Though it is available to all, it is given only to those who are ready.

- With each communication with divine spirit, we will discover more deeply who we truly are, who we have always been. We are truth-seekers.

- Our loved ones who dwell beyond this life have a divine mandate to help those of us still here on earth. It is their highest purpose and their most pristine cause. Through our communications with them and their messages to us, we can both evolve higher. We are aided by their wise counsel and unique perspective, and they are made brighter by their service to us. These beloved ones are always standing by, waiting for us to accept their continued existence and to bring them into our hearts.

Overcoming Adversity

- Our purpose as beings of light is to evolve to higher spirituality through the experiences of mortal life. This includes both the bitter and the sweet experiences.

- All of us will know adversity at some point in our lives. However, we will all experience different levels of it. Some will pass through major challenges, some only minor.

- We may think of adversity as a curse, but as we pass through it on this earthly sojourn, we will come to find that these painful experiences are the ones in which we grow and evolve most dramatically. They will refine us. And they will engender in us a deep and powerful appreciation for the sweet moments in life. Rather than a shack of shallowness and apathy, they will make of us a fortress of strength and wisdom. But we will become only as strong and enlightened as we choose to be. The choice is always our own.

- There are different types of adversity: There are challenges we bring upon ourselves such as addictions, chaos, inner turbulence, poor lifestyle choices, and self-destruction. These can be overcome. There are challenges brought upon us by others such as physical harm, abuse, or discrimination. These also can be overcome. Then there are those challenges that are unpreventable such as physical or mental disability, limitations, certain types of illness, or inherited challenges. Many of these must be endured, some throughout a lifetime, but we can rise above and transcend their effects. This is to be done in spirit.

- The first and most significant act in overcoming adversity is to acknowledge our position as divine beings on an eternal path, given the tools and help necessary to guide us safely through. Our belief in these tools is paramount to their effectiveness. Everyone has them, and each is given them specifically to meet his or her individual needs throughout this life. The gifts we come into mortal life with are as unique as each person born into this world, and were appointed with perfection and endless wisdom. Each of us must come to an acceptance and understanding of this.

- There will not be a soul who does not pass through adversity on some level, and so our comparisons to one another only serve to divide us. We are connected by an eternal bond and are thus a human family experiencing earth life together, as *one*. We were given one another to help, guide, teach, and strengthen us. Often times, the help is there in the form of support, encouragement, or example by another, but because we do not open our eyes and see, this help goes unrealized. This is the first phase of Separation.

- We are of infinite wisdom already, endowed with light and divinity and endless possibility. We have eons of experience and knowledge, and are capable of rising to unseen heights—far beyond anything we know of in this sphere. Our power and potential are unfathomable. The highest within us resides in us now, here, and is fully alive. We can tap into it at any time, or all the time, as we so choose. We need only open our eyes, our minds, our hearts, and accept it without doubt and without fear. We need only believe. When we disbelieve or doubt, or act in a way that is contrary to our highest, we lose a portion of this light—the spark of the divine—and our journey becomes more difficult. This is the second phase of Separation.

- We are the offspring of Ultimate Love. We are glorified children who are cherished, nurtured, and adored in heavenly realms. We are courageous angels of light who are held safely in the strong arms of Power and Wisdom. This Power is available to us like a lifeline that can never be broken. However, its capacity to help us is determined by our willing reception of it and our respect for its sacred nature. We know this Power. We have always known it. Some of us are utilizing this Power and moving forward and upward in our spiritual progress. And some of us have merely forgotten or rejected this Power. This is the third phase of Separation.

The true method of overcoming adversity, then, is *Connection*: First, connect with the human divine—our human family; Second, connect with the beings of light that we are—our own spirit identity; Third, connect with the Hand of Love and Compassion which reaches out to us every moment of every day throughout our lives. Our separation from these three is darkness. Our connection is infinite light. We must turn to each other, turn to the highest within us, and turn to the Light.

Acknowledgements

Igive my highest gratitude to my divine Father in Heaven whose guiding hand has made possible every moment of my life. For His peerless wisdom and matchless love, I am forever thankful.

I know for certain that my inspirations while writing this book were given by my mother, Carol. Beyond the grave, she was helping me to find the right words, to interpret my experiences through a divine filter, and to express them with a clarity and honesty only an angel can accomplish. She was, in the most literal sense, my "ghost writer." By her redeeming love, I live today.

To my spectacular children—Jaede, Quinn, Shale, Faith, and Psalm—I give joyful devotion. Their love and luminous lessons are the fire in my soul. To Dan, the man who loves me with ultimate cherishing, I give my heart. What a powerful gift he is.

I give gracious thanks to all of my beloved ones—on both sides of the veil. To all who bring light into my world and to all who light the way for me, your hope and sustaining support mean everything to me. I love the gifts you have shared and the time you have invested in our walk together.

Thank you.

I will be the kind of woman who makes a worthy recipient of your precious contributions. My life, work, and heart are a reflection of the light in you.

About the Author

LeeAnn Taylor is the mother of five children, three of whom were born with Fragile X syndrome, a genetic disorder causing profound mental impairment and the most common known cause of autism. These three children have been her greatest teachers and they continue to facilitate her most spiritual experiences. Her triumphant journey of courage, resilience, and redemption beyond the veil serves as the luminous foundation for her sacred work and is the inspiration behind her spiritual artistry.

As an award-winning independent filmmaker, spiritual writer, and personal mentor, LeeAnn teaches the eternal nature of humankind and the indomitable power of the soul. Her story and teachings are featured in magazine articles, online radio shows, women's networks, and luminary forums where she invites her fellowmen to reclaim their divine heritage and become waking angels. Driven by a profound gratitude for life, LeeAnn loves serving others. She uses her unique ability to transcend the veil in helping people overcome major challenges and turning them to a path of higher pursuit. She is a champion for hope and for the advancement of light. She also writes poetry, Celtic music, and is a devoted student of the Divine.

Propelled by an inspired vision for humanity, LeeAnn Taylor emerges as an original new voice of enlightenment. Her writings, wisdom, and works can be found at www.leeanntaylorstory.com.

LeeAnn's Next Book
Coming in 2014

LeeAnn Taylor's upcoming sequel, *Heavenly Messages from Earth*, reveals her sacred work with her disabled sons, Quinn and Shale. In this controversial new book, LeeAnn opens up and shares her intimate experiences as she begins communication with her sons' spirits, and then later as she is taken through the veil in an astounding encounter where she views them in their perfected state—without their disabilities. She is shown their ancient gifts, and shares their beautiful teachings, their mysterious wisdom, and their compelling message for humanity.

In answer to the promise made by her mother's spirit, LeeAnn was given divine knowledge regarding not only her sons' unique earthly mission, but also the higher path walked by all individuals with significant disabilities here in mortality. Here, for the first time, she introduces the sacred cause enjoined by her and her sons, and its far-reaching implications. She explores our path of wisdom as a human family, our inherent challenges and potential, and reveals how all of us—no matter our circumstance—can pierce the veil to communicate with the Divine firsthand in a two-way conversation.

Heavenly Messages from Earth is an intriguing spiritual journey through uncharted territory—a powerful pilgrimage into the mystical, yet very real, realm of heavenly beings—and a modern manual for the courageous truth-seeker.